I WAS A SOLDIER

SOLDIER

SURVIVAL AGAINST THE ODDS

My Autobiography

Necola Hall

HANSIB

First published in 2014
by Hansib Publications Limited

P.O. Box 226, Hertford, Hertfordshire, SG14 3WY
United Kingdom

www.hansibpublications.com

ISBN 978-1-906190-89-7

Printed in Great Britain

Dedication

I am very thankful for the family that I am so privileged to have. I dedicate this book to my three gorgeous children: Michael Jr, Makayla and Moriah, and to the special memory of my child who didn't make it – Hope Natania Hall – stillborn at twenty weeks' gestation.

This book could not be possible without the loving support of my wonderful husband, Michael.

Acknowledgements

My deepest thanks to my dear mother, Aldith Dixon, who has endured many hardships through the years and has taught me that I should never let go of my dreams.

Thanks also to all my siblings for all the times we shared as children – the good and the bad.

I am also grateful to Mrs Hyacinth Williams and family for their unselfish support over a long period of my life.

I am eternally grateful to my secondary school teacher, Mrs Joan Vickers, for her support and for being a role model to me.

With emotion, I wish to thank Sister Gwendolyn Thomas for always being at the other end of the line to listen and to guide me when I needed someone to talk to in confidence. I would also like to say a special thanks to church sisters Joyce Carr and Catherine Hall for being mother figures to me in England.

Thanks also to our friends Bobbette Marshall, Evangelist Dorrett Depass-Williams, Sis Thelma Pratt, Sis Rosalind Johnson, Bro Olloum and Minister Beverley Bulloumah, Rev Horace Bennett, Rev Barrington Laing, Bishop Horatio Fearon, Rev Raymond Veira, Rev Delroy Wilkins and Rev George Brown.

I owe a debt of gratitude to Arif Ali and the team at Hansib Publications. Thanks also to Jackie Raymond for her erudite proofreading.

I must say a big thank you to my wonderful husband, Michael, for believing in me, and for his constant prayers, love, support and encouragement.

And finally, thanks to all those who read this book. I pray that it is a blessing and an inspiration.

INTRODUCTION

How do I begin? This is not an easy task for me by any stretch of the imagination. I decided to write this book due to the many difficulties that I had experienced in my life. I remember sharing some of my testimonies with someone years ago, and the person suggested strongly that I write a book to inspire other people who perhaps were going through similar experiences. I thought at the time that this was extremely far-fetched for someone with my background to consider. This thought was further enhanced, though, during the time when I was receiving counselling for depression. I was required to write all that I had experienced, in order to get to the core of the issues that had affected me deeply.

It was at that point when I realised that the many difficulties of my childhood, growing up in Jamaica, had actually had a greater impact on me than I had previously thought or imagined. This exercise truly caused me to recognise that the circumstances of my childhood were a factor in how I had dealt with some of the issues in my adult life.

My siblings and I had an extremely difficult childhood, which is depicted throughout the story, but this served as an inspiration for me to break the cycle of poverty resulting from a lack of education. I was determined that, with the help of Jesus Christ, I would break this cycle.

I decided to come to the UK in search of a better life, and took the opportunity to join the British Army when it presented itself. It has been an honour to have served this great institution and to have worn its uniform with great pride. Sadly, though, some of my experiences were below what I had anticipated, but they have all contributed to me becoming a much stronger and resilient person.

Being in the British Army has had a lasting impact on me and has contributed to me realising many of my dreams, as a result I am extremely proud that I was a soldier.

1

I arrived at Heathrow Airport in London on March 7, 2002, having spent just over nine hours on the flight from Kingston, Jamaica. This was the first time I'd ever been on a plane, and it was also a very long and lonely journey, having left my husband, family and friends behind. There was a lot going through my mind the entire way, with lots of questions about myself, my future and this great unknown.

Having cleared Immigration, I was met by my family friends and former neighbours: Mrs Williams and her son, Paul, who now resided in London. When I arrived at the airport, it was far different from what I had expected. I was very surprised that there were no leaves on the trees; I remember remarking to myself that the trees were like 'sticks just standing'. It was the beginning of March and, to me having just arrived from Jamaica, it was bitterly cold. Anyway, I was on a mission and I decided to grit my teeth and press on.

It was on the National Express coach on the journey from Heathrow Airport to Bristol (where I would be staying with a friend) that the reality of leaving home to come to this great big country finally dawned on me: the magnitude of what I was embarking on; and the fact that I had just left my husband and the comfort of my home in a quest to improve myself. It was so difficult for me; I was very emotional and I started to cry. I began to question the wisdom of the decision to come in the first place. I started questioning why was my life like this and, very importantly, why did Michael allow me to come, and whether he really loved me. Or did he just want to get rid of me so he could pursue other women as, up until then, we had only been married just over two years.

The decision to come to England was not an easy one but, at the time, it seemed like the only way out for me. Over the years, I had seen family members, including my paternal grandfather and other relatives, emigrate from Jamaica to the 'mother land', and they seemed to have done well economically. Like them, this was now my reality.

I was twenty-five years old, with no formal education, and was faced with the situation where I was unemployed, due to having recently been made redundant from my job as a shop assistant in a mobile phone shop in Kingston. I had become increasingly frustrated at having to stay at home day after day in the hot house in Greater Portmore, St Catherine, where it was the norm for temperatures to be eighty-five degrees Fahrenheit – or even higher. I prayed to the Lord for a change in my circumstances, to either return to evening classes or to get another job, which was proving very difficult. I knew that I was a driven and ambitious individual, and that I wanted to make something of my life. In fact, I had always wanted to be a nurse, and thought that going to England would help me to realise this dream.

After being in the UK for about a week, I thought there was potential for me to survive and do well here, but I became increasingly sad due to the fact that Michael and I were living over four thousand miles apart. I missed my husband, my extended family, my mother and my home. The friends with whom I was staying in Bristol gradually became unfriendly and unhelpful, causing our relationship to deteriorate.

Michael and I would speak to each other every single day, sometimes at length and sometimes up to three times a day – which cost a lot in phone cards for both of us – but we seemingly did not care, as we just wanted to be speaking to each other all the time.

It didn't take very long for Michael to decide to leave his insurance sales job to join me. He had done very well, making the Million Dollar Round Table – the life insurance industry benchmark of success – in his first year of selling, and was looking forward to an even more successful second year.

To my utter delight and extreme joy, I went to pick Michael up at Gatwick Airport. I remember it was a cold and hazy April morning, but I did not mind about the weather, as the love of my life had joined me in England, and this made me extremely happy.

In one of our many telephone conversations that Michael and I had had, prior to him coming to the UK, he told me that the Lord had given him a few Scriptures from the book of Deuteronomy, Chapter 6, verses 10 to 12:

> When the Lord your God brings you into the land He swore to your fathers, to Abraham, Isaac and Jacob, to give you – a land with large, flourishing cities you did not build, houses filled with all kinds of good things you did not provide, wells you did not dig, and vineyards and olive groves you did not plant – then when you eat and are satisfied, be careful that you do not forget the Lord, who brought you out of Egypt, out of the land of slavery. (KJV)

Even before we were reunited in England, Michael and I prayed to God using these Scriptures, as we saw them as God's divine promises that He would provide and honour our faith in Him.

My uncle, Rev Michael Walker, had made provision for us to rent a flat from one of his church members in Battersea, London. This would have been shared accommodation, with several different people sharing the kitchen, bathroom, etc. However, having recently come to England from Jamaica, this sort of living arrangement was extremely strange to us, and I honestly didn't think we could have existed in this way. To be frank, I just didn't like London; at the time, it seemed very fast-paced, and the people seemed cold and unfriendly.

While sitting in the Arrivals waiting area at Gatwick Airport, waiting for the plane Michael was travelling on to arrive, I made the decision that I would tell Michael that we would be going to Birmingham with his cousin, with whom he had travelled from Jamaica. I hadn't asked his cousin if we could stay with him, nor did I have another plan if he had said he couldn't accommodate us. I knew that my grandad lived on Station Road in that city, but I had no other information as to which town or community. I had confidence, however, that the Lord would eventually work it out for us.

With the help of Michael's cousin, Peter, we bought our tickets for the National Express coach to Birmingham. It was a long and uncomfortable journey, but I was very happy because I was sitting next to my husband, and I was the happiest woman on earth.

The coach took about three and a half hours to get to the Birmingham coach station. I thought we would have gone straight home with Peter, but instead he told us to wait in the coach station for approximately fifteen to twenty minutes, and he would return with his brother, Morris, to pick us up. We waited over three hours for them to return. In the interim, we called Peter's phone without success, and were beginning to fear that we were going to be stranded at the coach station with nowhere to sleep. We watched many people come and go and started to despair, wondering why we had left Jamaica.

Michael decided to try Peter's number again, and he finally answered, stating, "Soon come, we are sorting somewhere for you to stay, at a bed and breakfast." At that time, I didn't even know what a 'bed and breakfast' was, but eventually they came and picked us up, and took us to the bed and breakfast, which was located in the Edgbaston area of the city. The brothers faithfully promised to pick us up in the morning, as they would now sort out somewhere for us to stay.

Peter and Morris came for us at about half past eleven the next morning, and took us to Peter's flat in the Aston area of the city. The flat had one bedroom with a bathroom and kitchen. It was typically untidy, and had a strong smell of tobacco scent. Peter graciously offered us his bed, while he stayed on the settee.

While we were at Peter's, we met some of Michael's relatives, namely Karl and his family, and later Roy and his family. Karl was over six feet tall and muscular; spoke very loudly most of the time. He was a real character, but I thought he was quite genuine and sincere. At one point, he gave us £20 and told us not to tell Morris and Peter.

Roy, Peter and Morris' brother, was quite different, however. He worked as an independent financial advisor, and lived in a leafy and affluent part of the West Midlands. He was married with two teenaged boys. Roy was a true inspiration to us, and seemed very considerate. He would make time to take us around the city of Birmingham and the adjoining areas. His younger son played tennis, and Roy would take us to his matches just as a way of showing us the quality of life we might be able to achieve, if we managed to settle in this country and had the ambition and drive to be successful. He showed us his own journey, by taking us to the house that his parents had bought in Handsworth, which was a deprived area in the city, and trailed his journey to where he currently resided.

He and his family gave us tremendous support: on several occasions he would give us groceries from their monthly market shopping at the Bull Ring; they also gave us money, and invited Michael and me to have dinner with them. We were very grateful for the help that Michael's cousins gave to us. Without them, our lives in this country would not have been possible.

It was important, though, for us to realise that while we lived at Peter's flat, this could only be a temporary arrangement; it became apparent to us that we were intruders, and were potentially hampering Pete's relationship with his girlfriend, now that the flat had become a bit overcrowded. I decided to try to locate my grandfather's house. With the help of an A-Z of Birmingham and, after having several supporting conversations with Peter and Morris, we set off from Aston to Handsworth, in search of Grandfather Dixon's house. I told myself that he had not been a father to my father, so this was his chance to redeem himself and make amends by supporting Michael and me – at least until we were settled. The search proved futile on this occasion; we failed to speak to anyone who knew the Dixon family from Station Road.

Another couple of weeks had passed, and we were beginning to become very desperate, having no money left, and still staying at Pete's flat. We started to feel like a burden to our dear cousins. I managed to call a cousin in Jamaica, who gave me a telephone number for Grandad Dixon.

I was quite nervous to call, but was encouraged by Michael to do so. So we went to a telephone box and made the call. His wife answered the phone.

"Hello," I said, nervously.

"Hello," she answered.

I then asked, "Is this the Dixon residence?"

"Yes," she said, in a quiet, assuring tone.

"This is Yvonne, Tony's daughter, grandfather's son from Jamaica," I said nervously.

"OK. I will get your grandfather for you."

My grandfather then came on the phone. After speaking for about a minute, I remembered I was calling from a public telephone box and that my credit was running out. He asked me for the number of the box and he rang me back. I told him of our situation, and he told me that I should call back the next day, which I did. Two days later, we arranged for my Uncle Arnold to take us to the home.

It was Friday afternoon when we were picked up by Arnold. I remembered thinking that he looked nothing like my dad, although he was equally tall, I thought. I then thought to myself that perhaps he resembled his mum. We arrived at the Station Road address and, to our surprise, the house was filled with people: grandad and my step-grandmother (who is known as Ibbi, but we affectionately called her Grandma); grandad's brother and his wife were there, with one of their daughters. Also present were Floyd, my other uncle, and one of my cousins, whose father was another of my uncles, who I learnt had died in a motor vehicle accident when he was a teenager.

The atmosphere felt really tense; everybody tried to be friendly, it seemed, but there was a sense of insincerity that I picked up from the questions that we were being asked. We were very respectful to everyone, and tried as best as possible to accommodate all the questions. In a sense, I could understand the line and intensity of the questioning as, to a large extent, we were strangers. Here I was with my husband, looking for a place to stay, with a grandfather that I hardly knew – only having met once before, when I was a child on one of his visits to Jamaica. I sensed deep down that I harboured some resentment towards my grandad, as I felt that he was largely responsible for the difficult upbringing that my father had had.

They agreed for us to stay with them until we had enough money to find somewhere for ourselves. I had mixed emotions about all that was happening around us; however, on the one hand, there was relief that we were getting somewhere to stay that we didn't have to pay rent for, while, on the other hand, I was deeply uncomfortable about bringing my husband into this type of set-up.

I felt, though, that we had common ground in our Christian faith: Arnold and Grandma Ibbi were strong Methodists – Arnold, as I understood it, was a Methodist minister for two churches in the Greater Manchester and Liverpool areas, and Ibbi could be described as a faithful mother in the local church. With Michael and I being devoted Christians ourselves, there seemed to be area of agreement.

That same Friday evening, Arnold took us to the 'chippy' (a fish and chips takeaway) near to the house, and told us we could order a meal for each of us. I had fish and chips and a soda, and Michael had the same. We took the food back home, and thoroughly enjoyed it. We spent the rest of the evening chatting and getting to know my grandad and his family.

2

Although our faith in Jesus Christ was very important, I only managed to attend church for the first time in this country approximately seven weeks after Michael arrived. We were so unsettled to the extent that, unfortunately, going to church was not our main priority at the time. Although Grandma Ibbi and Arnold were influential members of the Methodist church, at no time had we even considered attending their church, as we were of the Church of the Firstborn denomination in Jamaica, and we were intent on continuing in that denomination.

Before Michael and I were married, I attended God's Way Assembly in Jamaica. We had agreed that we would have our wedding ceremony at my church, then I would join him in worshipping at Church of the Firstborn. Both Michael and I received glowing references from our dear Pastor in Jamaica, Rev Horace Bennett, and we were given the phone number of a church brother, who had made the move to England a few months before us. We eventually got in touch with him, who then directed us to a sister who attended a branch of the church in Erdington, Birmingham. We rang and spoke to this lady, who sounded so reassuringly calm and caring. This was Friday and, by Sunday, we had been picked up and were attending church.

The church was evidently a small congregation, with predominately older brethren and a few younger people; the majority of the younger ones had recently come over from Jamaica, as we had. It gave us a sense of belonging and security, and we quickly got involved in many of the activities. We were committed in attending as regularly as possible, and built good relationships with most of the members. The membership at that time was approximately thirty. The church was led by the elderly Pastor Prentice, who never failed to bring Michael and me a loaf of whole wheat bread and who placed several pound coins into our hands on many occasions. Michael often remarked that this was the Lord taking care of us.

Attending church gave us the opportunity to network with the younger people in the church, and we were inspired to take on new challenges that would ultimately contribute to a better quality of life for us in this country. We were introduced to one of the community schools in the deprived inner city area of Lozells. I decided to sign up at the college to do a Certificate course in Computer Software. Michael too wanted to start at the college, but couldn't due to the lack of finances, so we decided that, since Michael had a better academic background than I, then I should go ahead, and he could start later as and when things improved for us.

We gradually got very close to the sister who had come and picked us up for church. She turned out to be as caring and as sensitive as she had sounded on the telephone the first time we spoke to her. Her name was Vera Gregory. One Sunday after church, she came over to me and asked, "Sister Nicole, would you like a job?"

"Yes," I answered stutteringly, with adrenalin running down my spine. Within a few seconds, I felt a sense of hope that God was about to make a way for us; I didn't even consider what type of job this could be.

However, Sister Gregory continued, "I own a care home business, and wondered if you would be interested in doing a couple of hours for a couple of days during the mornings."

"Yes, that would be great," I said, more confidently this time. She went on to give me the address of her care home.

I had no inclination at all that this very polite, petite, unassuming lady had any sort of business and, furthermore, that she wanted me to work for her. I was very delighted (to say the least), and this gave us great hope that soon things would get better. I was allowed to work twenty hours on my visa, so I worked around my classes. By the end of the week, I received an envelope with, I recall, about £67 and a few pence. This gave us such a good feeling of hope and independence.

A couple of months after I had started attending college, they had a careers day there, and several businesses and organisations came to make presentations to recruit prospective apprentices and employees, including the British Army. I attended, and I was particularly interested in hearing what the Army recruiters had to say. The information was expertly presented, and had me thinking of the possibilities, especially due to the fact that I had always wanted to be in uniform. Several years before, soon after leaving St Andrew Technical High School in Jamaica, I had actually signed up to join the police force; I did the entrance test but, unfortunately, was unsuccessful. This was devastating for me, and it took me some time to recover from the disappointment. To be honest, Michael had to encourage me time and again. I eventually lifted myself, and was determined to be in uniform, so I attempted to join the Jamaica Defence Force (JDF). I did not get the chance to enlist, however, as it was extremely difficult to get in. This was due to the high demand for the few places whenever they became available, and to the fact that it was even more difficult for females; they told me that there would not be another batch of women intake for the next two years, as I had just missed the most recent intake.

In my mind, this potential opportunity presented by the British Army seemed too good to be true. I was both excited and nervous at the same time. Excited, due to possibilities that this opportunity with the Army could mean, and nervous about whether or not I would actually pass the recruitment process.

The information given by the Army recruiters was, in my little world, virtually mind-blowing. They stated that, since Michael and I were married, if successful in the recruitment process we would be given a house immediately after basic training, together with a list of other fringe benefits that sounded just amazing. In addition, we would be paid around £12,000 per annum. At that time, we always converted sterling to Jamaican dollars, in order to make a comparison. In 2002, that would have been around 660,000 in Jamaican dollars, which would have been a decent income if we had received this in Jamaica. I was aware that this was not a realistic comparison by any means, given the marked differences in the economies of both countries, but we did it anyway.

Both Michael and I submitted our documentation, and we began in earnest to get our fitness up to the required standard. Time was swiftly running out for Michael, however; he had put on a bit of weight, and he was fast approaching the cut off age for entry into the Army. He was bitterly devastated when he was told by the recruiter at the Birmingham recruitment office that he would no longer be considered for the Army due to his age.

We were disappointed at this news, but I decided that I would continue to pursue my dream of becoming a soldier. My life became more intense; it became difficult to live with my grandparents, as they decided that they could not carry us any longer, and technically we were forced out.

To be fair, this was understandable; we had come to their home unannounced, and they had been gracious in helping us in our dire time of need. We are eternally grateful for their love and support – especially Grandma Ibbi. They were even good enough to pay the first month's rent for the flat that we rented.

Life became more challenging for me. I had to be juggling my time between attending college, working and training to improve my fitness. If I attended classes in the morning, for example, I then went to work in the afternoon, and would go running in the evening whatever the weather. On one occasion, Michael and I ran through snow – four inches deep – but I was motivated to attain the fitness levels no matter what.

The time came for me to do the British Army Recruit Battery (BARB) Test. I was a little nervous, but pretty confident that I would be successful because, unlike the Jamaica Police recruitment process, the Army gave us practice tests, and I had been scoring quite highly on all of them. I had done the test electronically, and learnt within minutes of completing it that I had been successful.

The grade that I received meant that I was qualified to join several different trades, including chef, signals, clerk and supplier. I chose to join supplier, as I imagined that this would have been the easiest for me to handle, and would help me enjoy my future Army career.

I told my career officer of my choice of wishing to be a supplier. He confirmed that a place was available, and the next stage was to be the dreaded selection process. This was primarily a series of tests, which usually ran for the period of two days at one of the selection centres. The test included a thorough medical examination: my greatest challenge of all – the 1.5-mile run, which I would need to complete in 14 minutes (for females); team-building tasks, as well as a grenade-throwing test; information retention test and, finally, an interview with the selection officer.

My first selection took place in Lichfield in the West Midlands. I say first because, in pursuit of my dream to become a soldier, I eventually attended three selections.

The first at Lichfield did not go according to plan at all. I was focused, used my initiative and tenacity throughout all the stages, and personally thought I had done a very good job, but was left absolutely devastated when I was told that I had not been successful on this occasion. Initially I cried uncontrollably, but it did not take very long to rebuild my resolve, and to be determined that I would return; the next time I would do everything in my power to ensure that I was successful. The unsuccessful recruits were told that we had to wait six months before returning.

I went to back college and carried on attending classes normally but, now that I had been introduced to the Army, I became almost fixated on joining, due to the opportunities that were promised at the careers day.

It was getting increasingly harder for us being on our own in Birmingham. I spoke to a friend who lived in Bristol, and who had also come over from Jamaica. She had rented a house in the Avonmouth area of that city, and encouraged us to move down to Bristol. I wasn't sure at first that this was such a good idea, but Michael and I discussed it at length and later decided to go. I was told by the recruitment officer in Birmingham that I should be able to continue with the recruitment process in Bristol.

Michael and I packed all our belongings into our suitcases and bags, including pots and pans, books and all sorts. The trouble was that we had no transportation to take us, so we bought a couple of coach tickets on National Express. We took a taxi down to Digbeth coach station, and struggled to take all our bags into the station. We noticed that a number of the fellow passengers were staring at us. When the coach arrived, the driver helped to put our belongings into the luggage compartments, stating that, if he had known that we had so much luggage, he would not have allowed us to travel. Michael and I were not too bothered about people and their opinions, however, as we were determined to survive these early days in this country. We knew that with the help of Jesus Christ things would get better.

Bristol seemed quieter and more relaxed in comparison to London and Birmingham; it felt a lot more rural, which was very much to my liking.

Michael accompanied me to the recruitment office in the city centre. We went in and spoke to a recruitment officer, who gave us some disturbing information. He told us that, unfortunately, I had to start the recruitment process all over again, as this was a different city, and they operated differently to their colleagues in Birmingham. I questioned why this was the case, but he only reiterated what he had said before. This meant that I had to do the BARB Test all over again, as well as supplying all the documentation I had previously submitted. After hearing all that the recruitment officer had said, there were a lot of questions in my mind, such as why not just give up, and stop pursuing this elusive dream of becoming a soldier in the British Army? But I soon thought to myself that everything worth achieving was worth fighting for, and I had never envisaged myself as a quitter – no matter what the odds were against me. With this steely determination, I decided that I would press on, and even adopted this mantra: "Let them refuse me, I will not refuse them."

A couple of weeks later, I sat the BARB Test again and, once again, I did quite well. I still opted for supply specialist. There was a twist, however, as I was informed that the Bristol recruitment office didn't just send you directly to selection when you met the Body

Mass Index (BMI) requirement, and could do the 1.5 miles in fourteen minutes or less (for females). No, they would first send you for a locally-organised pre-selection in Chepstow, which you had to pass before they recommended you to be put forward for selection. This was even more stressful for me but, again, I motivated myself to be determined to achieve this goal. Yes I cried, and yes it was painful, but I believed in the Scripture that says: 'I can do all things through Christ, who strengthens me' (Philippians 4:13 NKJV).

Pre-selection for the Bristol recruitment office was done on a Saturday; all the recruits had to arrive by 7.00 am. I remember that it was a very bright and cold day in January. The wind was blustery, which made it seem even colder. I was feeling extremely nervous but very confident that I was going to pass, as I had been training every day to make sure that I met the required fitness criteria.

We boarded the coach and went over to South Wales. It was a long day, but I was quite happy as I had done well, and was commended for my effort. This wasn't the case for some of the other recruits, however, as many had failed the pre-selection and there was a lot crying, especially from the female recruits.

I returned home and continued with what I considered to be intense training: running along the Portway, which is a major arterial road, which runs from Avonmouth through Shirehampton and down to the city centre. This was a scenic route, to run along the Gorge with the high rocks on one side and the beautiful picturesque views of the historic Bristol suspension bridge on the other. On a clear day, it would be great to be out running. I really enjoyed this. The selection was now three weeks away.

Time seemed to progress so slowly that Michael and I were getting frustrated. On one occasion, we even had an argument; I can't even remember what it was about. I am sure it was about something very minor, but at the time it seemed major. The time for me to go and have a run approached, but I noticed that Michael did not move; we would normally run together. I didn't allow this to deter me, however, so I got dressed and left him in the house. That is how determined I was.

The date for the selection finally arrived, and I was told that the selection would once again be at the Lichfield Selection Centre in the West Midlands. I was issued with travel warrants, and told by the recruitment officer that I would have to make my way there by train. I was very excited, because I knew that I had prepared very well and felt that my previous bitter disappointment had given me a gritty determination to be successful. The journey to Lichfield was quite adventurous; I boarded the train at Bristol Temple Meads up to Birmingham New Street, then changed to a train to Lichfield. From there, all the recruits and I were picked up by coach, which took us to the recruitment centre. This time, the place did not seem so intimidating – for obvious reasons. This time, I knew what to expect. By the end of the selection, I felt confident that I had done very well. This was confirmed by the selection officer, who informed me that I had passed the selection. I was ecstatic with joy; I felt relieved more than anything, now that my Army career could get started.

Approximately two weeks after selection, I received a letter outlining Phase 1 training. I was told that the training would take place at a barracks in Pirbright, Surrey. Again I was very excited, and couldn't wait to get there. I continued with my training at home, as I did not want to lose fitness and be at a disadvantage when I began basic training.

I was to get one of the greatest shocks of my life thus far, however. Just as I thought that I was now on my way to start training in the Army, there was a turn of events that I just did not anticipate. I received a call to go into the recruitment office. The information given was certainly not expected. The recruitment officer told me that he had been made aware that there was no place available for a supply specialist, so I was no longer required to attend basic training at Pirbright. Furthermore, there would not be an intake of supply specialists for the next year, as there had been an over-subscription in that trade. Stuttering in disbelief at what I was hearing, I asked softly, "Do I have to wait one year?"

"Yes," he replied, sternly.

I then said to him, "OK then, I'll wait."

"No," he told me. "The Army needs recruits, and we are not able to allow you to hang around for one year."

"OK," I said. "I will choose another trade. I could do Chef, then!" I proposed.

"No," he said. "All RLC trades are currently over-subscribed for the next year."

There and then I decided that I had to look at the other career options available to me in the Army. Since I had done reasonably well on the BARB Test, the options available to me were signals, nursing and clerk. My final decision was to become a clerk. I informed the recruiter of my decision; he, however, turned to me and said, "You will have to do the selection all over again, including the BARB Test." To be honest, I couldn't believe what I was hearing. It was very distressing, and my response to him was, "So why is this? I've already passed the selection with a good score; I've already passed the BARB Test with a good score; why am I experiencing this?" I started sobbing. I didn't know how to deal with this, and I was feeling confused and rejected.

This latest situation was totally unexpected, and had a negative impact on me. This was such a harsh and painful experience, but there was no movement on the part of the recruiter, so I decided that, once again, I had come too far to be disappointed like this, and had to muster up the strength to carry on. I was feeling a deep hurt, but was motivated to continue in pursuit of my dream to join the Army.

On arrival home from the careers office, I was totally distraught and began to cry. Michael was very upset at the way I had been treated, and told me that I shouldn't bother to humiliate myself any further. I understood exactly what Michael was getting at, as he knew the hard work that I had invested in achieving this goal. It just seemed so unfair that they claimed that they couldn't use the results of the most recent BARB Test and selection scores in submitting my application into the Adjutant General's Corps, especially since these results were very current.

I heard and understood what Michael had said but, on reflection the next morning, what was happening to me seemed very personal, and again I reminded myself that I would never allow any individual to undermine my ambition to achieve what I had set out to do. The disappointment lingered, but I was a driven individual, so I decided to continue with the process. I knew that my persistence and determination would pay off in the end. I then contacted the Bristol recruitment office, and asked the careers officer what would be the next stage in my ongoing recruitment into the British Army. He informed me that there would be a pre-selection the following week. Considering that I had already been to a pre-selection and selection only a few weeks before was a jolt to the system, so I had to depend on my inner strength and faith in Jesus Christ to remain focused. Michael was a constant support throughout this ordeal and, once I had made the decision to continue, he supported me wholeheartedly.

Again, I went on the pre-selection, and approached it with seriousness and commitment, as I did not want to take anything for granted which might have caused me to fail. The final day, I was told that I was successful and would be put forward for selection to enter into the Adjutant General's Corps, which dealt with soldiers' administration.

A few weeks later, I went to the full selection, again at the Lichfield Selection Centre. The hurt and pain of going again to do the same thing all over – having already passed it a few weeks earlier – was quite raw. A feeling of heaviness permeated my entire body, but at no time did I allow myself to be in a state of self-pity; I held on to the hope that anything worth achieving was worth fighting for.

After a couple of weeks, I received a letter from the Bristol careers office to attend the swearing in ceremony. It seemed that this was a big occasion, as I was told to dress smartly, which essentially meant that I should dress in my best office attire, which I did. The ceremony was quite a short one, but had an air of grandeur. The swearing of allegiance meant that from that day onwards, my life effectively belonged to the Army. It took approximately six weeks further for me to be called in for basic training.

I received my travel warrant to travel down to Winchester. Again, I was both nervous and excited: nervous because this was all new to me, and I knew it would be challenging. I was aware that the objective was to transform me from civilian to soldier, and they could be really rigid and robust. I was excited, too, as this was a proud moment in my life; I was very happy that I was finally on my way to becoming a soldier.

Michael accompanied me on the journey from Bristol Temple Meads to Winchester, which made it much easier for me. We arrived quite early at the station in Winchester and, just as we exited the station, there was a minivan parked across from the station, with signs marked "ATR Winchester" stuck to the windows. I went over and spoke to the driver, who stated that he was going on camp in about fifteen minutes. 'Great,' I thought to myself. This gave me enough time to say Goodbye to Michael. We had our last hugs and little kisses; he gave me a few words of encouragement, and we said our final Goodbye. I boarded the minivan and tried to make friends almost straightaway. I could see Michael watching the van until it was out of sight.

On arrival at camp, I felt a few butterflies in my stomach. I only felt a little better after I had been introduced to the other recruits and we had been taken to our accommodation. We later did quite a lot of paperwork. The following day, we did our medical, which included getting a vaccination. This was an ordeal for me; the medics had a very hard time getting my blood, as it was difficult to find my veins, so much so, that I was told to return in two weeks. We were then issued with our uniforms, after being briefed by a Lieutenant Colonel.

The next few weeks in training proved both challenging and rewarding. I tried my very best to keep up with both the physical and academic aspects of military training. I applied myself, and tried to get along with everyone as much as possible. I understood that the trainers could be very aggressive and direct, but I did not take any aggravations that came my way personally. To my advantage also was the bond formed with a number of other young people, who also came from Jamaica and other Caribbean and African countries, such as St Lucia, St Vincent, Ghana, Malawi and Fiji, to mention a few. It was evidently clear that there was a distinct division amongst the girls based on race. The White girls would sit by themselves, and we did likewise. It seemed to us – and we girls chatted about this on a few occasions – as if they wanted us to always be making the considerable effort to socialise outside the established groups. I made a reasonable attempt to interact with them, but it didn't seem that many of the White recruits reciprocated this gesture, so I just blocked this out as much as I possibly could, and carried on as normally as possible. I tried to support others when they were team leader no matter what their race, but found that when we Black recruits were leading, the support was not forthcoming.

On one particular day, the first session was swimming, and the corporal in charge of the session asked for swimmers and non-swimmers to form two groups. What happened next was interesting. Only one of the recruits originating from this country came into the non-swimmers' group. This was remarkably ironic, as the majority of us in the non-swimmers' group were from tiny islands surrounded by the beautiful Caribbean Sea. Where I came from, in Jamaica, a place called Bull Bay (approximately eleven miles from the capital, Kingston), you literally have to pass the sea each time you leave the house, in order to go shopping in Kingston or its environs. In fact, I could look at the sea from my parents' house. My only explanation as to why most of us could not swim was that, like mine, our parents may have been very protective of us, regarding the dangers of drowning at sea and, being a third world country, there was no money available to finance public pools.

We soon reached the halfway point of our basic training. This was an important stage, where our military and physical skills would be assessed. I did the one-and-a-half mile run in twelve minutes and twenty-eight seconds. I thought it was a good effort, but it was obvious that my troop commanders disagreed. I was excited to go on 'half way', which was an extended time in the field to hone our military skills; this was a highlight for us recruits. I was all packed and ready, when I was told that I had been 'back-squadded'. This was a terrible shock to me, as it now meant that I would have to go back two weeks to week five of basic training. This was difficult for me to understand, as I had finished the one-and-a-half mile run before many of the other recruits, who had not been back-squadded; it just did not seem right.

After being back-squadded at the halfway point, I was well received by my new troop, and I once again motivated myself to press on in order to achieve my goal.

Time progressed, and I gradually became more confident and assertive, and just didn't look back. The weeks elapsed so quickly that it was soon time for the passing out parade. This was what I called 'super exciting': the preparation and the anticipation gave me an exhilarating feeling; I just wanted the day to come and pass, so that I could go home and have a good time with Michael. I also wanted to go on to the Phase 2 training, where I could go home every weekend when I was not on guard duty.

The day of the passing out parade was a typical winter's day in February. It was pouring down with rain and freezing cold but, with the adrenalin flowing, the weather did not seem to matter much to me, as there was a lot to keep me focused on getting through the drills and activities for the day. In the end, it was a celebration, and I had a sense of personal victory and achievement. This might not have seemed a lot to others but, to me, this was a significant achievement, given the personal circumstances and struggles in my life thus far. I looked very smart in my Number 2 uniform, and I felt extremely proud of myself, as I had achieved this milestone by the help of Almighty God. I was now a soldier.

I believe we had a week's break after passing out, before we started our Phase 2 training. This was undertaken at Worthy Down, again in Winchester. This was a more civilised environment; it was not as regimental as basic training, but I had to be disciplined and apply myself well in order to get through successfully. If I am being honest, going to see Michael was the highlight of my weeks. I tried to get away as early as possible on a Friday, in order to catch the earliest train to Bristol as, with such limited time, every minute spent together was important. Michael always met me in the city centre, so our weekends together started at the bus stop in town. Looking back now, it struck me that, despite the time spent away on training, whenever I came home we never missed going to church together. I believe God has honoured this commitment.

Nine weeks went swiftly by, and I completed my training as a military clerk and was ready for my first posting. I chose to serve with the now defunct Scottish regiment, 1 Black Watch (Highland regiment) – an infantry regiment that was stationed in Warminster, Wiltshire during 2004. I chose this regiment primarily because on the map it seemed like the closest regiment to Bristol with a vacancy for a junior clerk. However, on the final day before leaving Worthy Down, we had an inspection by the Adjutant, who came round with other officers. She spoke to each of us and asked us where we were being posted to.

"1 Black Watch," I replied. They all gave a sarcastic chuckle.

She then added, "I hope you enjoy your time there." I thought to myself, 'What am I getting into?'

From their reaction, I felt that it might have been a wrong decision to choose this regiment. I made the decision, however, to remain close to Bristol, as I had developed an affinity for the city, and we had also developed close relations with members of the church we attended. I thought to myself that the decision had already been made, and I would just give it my best shot and see what happens. Perhaps they were just overreacting.

5

We left Phase 2 training on the Friday, and I was told that I had to be in work the following Monday morning. This meant that I had to go to camp on Saturday to sort out my Army quarters. I had to live on camp temporarily while the promised married quarters near the barracks were been prepared, as I lived too far to travel to work on a daily basis, and I didn't drive. I took the train over to Warminster, which took approximately forty-five minutes from Bristol, and arrived there about midmorning. On approaching the gate, I saw a Black private in full uniform in the guardroom. She had the same cap badge as mine. 'She's a clerk!' I remarked to myself. I wasn't sure of her country of origin at first, but it did not take long for me to find out. She spoke, and straightaway I knew that she was a Jamaican, too. Her strong Jamaican accent was pronounced, but was reassuring to hear. I was comforted that I had someone from my country around.

Her name was Cheyenne, and in a few short moments we were in conversation as if we had known each other for a long time. I tried to glean as much information as possible from her about the regiment, and what it was like living in that town. She informed me that there were three other Jamaican females attached to the regiment: another clerk, Shelley, and two chefs. This was positive to hear as far as I was concerned as, coming from Jamaica, it was important for me to have people around who understood each other, and to whom I could relate outside of work.

The girls took very good care of me over the weekend, showing me around the barracks and the town. We went to the different shops, etc. I should quickly add that there wasn't a lot to see in a market town, with its economy strongly dependent on the presence of the barracks. Over the weekend, we had all our meals together in the canteen, and I quickly struck up a good rapport with all of them; I was very happy to have their support.

I met up with the Jamaican clerk girls, and we walked down to the regimental headquarters (RHQ) together. I should have been there at 8.00 am, and made sure I turned up much in advance of that time. I paraded with HQ Company, immediately after that, I met up with the regimental administrative officer (RAO) who was the senior manager for the clerks, and the Detachment commander, also known as the Det commander, who was the second in command. They outlined my duties and where I would be working.

After training, I knew I would now be working with a Scottish regiment, but did not realise that it would be so difficult to understand their accent and diction. Coming from Jamaica, this was quite a shock to me because, as far as I could remember, I had not heard a Scottish person speak before, and now I was working around hundreds of them. In the main, I understood most of what they said, even though it took a few seconds after the person spoke for it to register in my brain. On the flip side, however, whenever the other Jamaican girls and I spoke together, we were almost certain that our Scottish colleagues equally did not understand us.

The first full week of my Army career went by quite quickly; I had so much to do, putting into practice all the theory that I had learnt in training, as well as getting to know my way around the regiment. I was an eager and willing soldier fresh out of training, who wanted to make a good impression to my immediate bosses and carry out my duties professionally, whilst conducting myself in a dignified and respectable manner. I had always wanted to be in uniform, and now that I had achieved my goal, I was determined to be the best at what I did.

I started to learn about the different characters I had to interact with on a daily basis: some were interesting, and others just got on with their jobs with no fuss at all. One of the big characters in the Detachment was a female staff sergeant; she appeared to be the one calling all the shots. To me, it seemed that many of the bigger decisions within the Det were made by her, and I say this because it seemed as if the Det Commander at the time was literally afraid of her. I got the impression that she always instigated or initiated matters, and everyone just seemed to go along with it.

Weeks in the job turned into months. I thought that by now I would have been able to demonstrate the skills I had learnt in training. Instead, I was not placed in a squadron, but worked with the documentation clerk and being the RHQ's unofficial 'runner'. I was extremely frustrated at this, as it did not enable me to develop my clerical skills. I also found that, in a setting where there was a pool of us in a large office, I was the one who was always tasked with serving the soldiers, no matter what I was doing, even if the other 'favoured' private soldier was also present. Being new in the Det, and wanting to prove my worth, caused me to be diligent in carrying out such unfair instructions. This was the Army, and I soon realised that, for some, there was no level playing field.

News started circulating in the battalion that we were to go to Iraq with the first set of soldiers, due to be dispatched in just over seven weeks' time. This was all confirmed by the commanding officer in a briefing that took place on the parade square. To be frank, when I was in training we were being prepared for this potential occurrence by our trainers at Worthy Down, but when the news came that I might actually be going to war, I felt a sense of numbness. The 1 Black Watch was an infantry battalion, and their policy was that everyone in the battalion had to go into 'theatre' (a major area of military activity). I was nervous at first, but gained confidence, as we had received the training in preparation for war.

While all this was happening in my professional life, Michael and I were faced with a serious domestic challenge. When Michael came to England, he was a life insurance sales representative, and had earned very good money over the previous year, by Jamaican economic standards. This might have influenced the immigration officer's decision not to put a stamp in his passport with the date for him to leave the UK. He unwittingly thought this was an indefinite leave visa. The whole situation with Michael's immigration status started unravelling when he received a letter from the Home Office, informing him that he had to leave the country within fourteen days of the date of the letter. I decided to be upfront with the Army, informing them of his situation. This was a stressful time for me to say the least, to be preparing to go into theatre in Iraq, and my husband having to return to Jamaica to reapply to re-enter the UK.

The Welfare department at the Black Watch gave helpful support. The welfare officer there was very resourceful and considerate. He used the power of his office, and gave Michael letters, which helped him to get the visa in Jamaica. Michael received the visa within two weeks of his return to Jamaica, and returned two weeks later, after spending time with his mother. That only left two weeks before I had to go to a war zone in Iraq. Doing this for the first time was an extremely tense time for us.

It seemed, however, that the situation regarding Michael's immigration situation was, as they say in Jamaica, 'town talk' within the Detachment, and I noticed a ratcheting up of hostilities towards me from certain senior members, since they knew what was taking place with us. One afternoon, a few days before Michael returned to Jamaica, I went home to have my lunch, as it was a short walk from the office. I had been home for about ten or fifteen minutes; I had had a bite to eat, and was sitting on the settee, watching the lunchtime news, when I heard a knock at the door. To our surprise, it was two female staff sergeants, the two female supervisors in the Detachment. We were quite suspicious of their visit, but I thought that they were being supportive. With Michael's imminent return to Jamaica, to regularise his immigration status, to our utter shock, the actual reason for their visit was to come and ask me to hand over my passport to them. I was left almost speechless at this request. This was unreal. 'What is happening here?' I thought to myself. They said the reason they were doing this was because they thought that I would go AWOL to Jamaica with Michael. This was totally unnecessary, as I was quite new in a job I had fought so hard to get into. My simple question was, "Why would I ever even think of doing such a stupid thing, as running away to Jamaica with my husband?" To me, this was such an abuse of power, that the relationship between these two and I deteriorated, but this was a challenge I would have to meet head on. I indeed handed over my passport, which was given back to me on Michael's return.

Michael managed to secure a reasonably good job as a stock controller at a medical supplies company in Bristol. It was a fair way to travel five days a week, but he was just grateful he had a job. On the other hand, however, the preparation to go to Iraq continued for me in earnest. The clerks, as all the other soldiers, were required to spend long hours in training for the battalion's imminent tour of Iraq but, as the time approached, I remained calm but anxious at the prospect of going into a war zone so soon after coming out of training.

The dreaded day finally came for us to go to Iraq. We had had our briefing the day before, and we were all set. I did all my final checks, and packed away my belongings. It was a very long night for the both of us; Michael and I watched as the electronic clock marked every hour in the darkness. I got out of bed at about 4.00 am. Michael and I had our Bible devotion together; we prayed, and asked for Christ's protection, so that I could return home 'in one piece', so to speak.

I left home quite early. Michael took me over to the camp, where a number of coaches were parked on the parade square. There was a buzz in the atmosphere, mixed with apprehension and some tears; wives and husbands and parents and partners said their goodbyes; some may have experienced this before, but for many like us, it was our very first time of separation, where one of us was going directly into harm's way, within reach of the enemy.

Michael stayed as long as he could; we hugged and kissed, and then he went. I was very confident that I would return home alive, even though there was that niggling thought that anything could happen even though, as a female and a clerk, I would not be confronting the enemy directly. All British soldiers going on a tour of duty had to write a will, just in case we did not return alive. For me, this highlighted the real gravity of the job, and the risks involved in being a soldier. I travelled up to the airport on the coach, sitting quite pensively, reflecting on my life and holding onto the faith that I would be back safely.

6

The flight time to Kuwait was approximately six and a half hours. We travelled during the night hours – I assumed that the commanders took this decision so as not to make us sitting targets for the enemy. I couldn't sleep at all, as many things were going through my mind: I missed Michael and the comfort and security that my husband gave. I was up for the trip, though, as much as I realistically could have been, as I understood the nature of soldiering.

After arriving in Kuwait, we took another plane to Basra Airport. From there, some thirty of us boarded a Chinook helicopter; it was the first time being in a Chinook for me. The engines thundered on loudly, as we sat silently in the dark. There were absolutely no lights on, in order to make sure we were not conspicuous to the enemy. There was utter silence in the aircraft, apart from the roaring engines; there was neither boyish bantering nor laughter. It seemed that everyone was quite focused and alert to the potential dangers surrounding us. We arrived on Camp Shaibah in the early hours of the morning, and I was struck by how hot the place was; Jamaica is hot, but that heat was like nothing I had experienced before.

During that same day, we were shown our accommodation and given a brief tour of the camp. Our tent was all girls, from all different cap badges. Some of the major American fast food establishments were in the little military town nearby, including Pizza

Hut and Subway. This was quite exciting; even though we were on the business of war, we had access to some familiar guilty pleasures. This gave us something exciting to look forward to – a kind of comfort away from home. Even though I am a born again Christian, hearing the sound of Bob Marley's music being played in the shuttle bus (which took us from camp to the shopping area) had me smiling. Deep down, I was quite happy to hear the music of my countryman being played in a faraway land.

There were times, however, when we had to be very alert and circumspect. We were mortared on several occasions; one night, we had to sleep in our helmets, as rockets were falling within 100 meters of camp. This was quite scary, as I saw my whole life flash in front of me; it was nerve-racking. Also, at one point, they told us to go inside a shipping container to take cover, but I didn't like that idea at all. I thought to myself that if an RPG (rocket-propelled grenade) hit the container, we would not stand a chance of surviving. Thank God that none did.

My greatest fear, however, was when the guys were going out on patrol. When I looked into their mainly youthful eyes, I saw fear; however, that fear, in my opinion, was superseded by an atmosphere of camaraderie and brotherhood that I only saw in this type of environment. Whenever I looked at them as they prepared to go out, my question to myself was, 'How many would not return alive?' This was hard as, like all of us, they had mothers and fathers, or spouses or children or siblings who loved and cared for them, and whose lives would have been totally devastated if the worst were to happen; this was hard.

It wasn't long after I had arrived when we had our first casualty. I believe he was a sergeant, who was married with two children. As clerks, we would be the first to know the details; this was a sad time for all. The battalion was very sombre but, as soldiers, we held together and pressed on. I'd never seen such determination in the guys; there was no longer fear, but grit and resolve that, while in theatre, they would carry out the job at hand, with the utmost bravery and professionalism.

In Iraq, we had to perform our usual clerical tasks, as well as our continuous training. I completed my Class 2 course while there. We had to do guard duty as well, which brought us into contact with the locals, some of whom worked on base as cleaners. This was when I felt most vulnerable: being on guard at the gate, as one never knew if the insurgents would be brazen enough to blow themselves up while you checked the purpose and legitimacy of their visit on camp.

Two weeks into the tour, I started to get acclimatised to the place, and having Cheyenne and Shelley there made things much easier. It was quite ironic that, just as it seemed that I was getting acclimatised, I became sick. I went to the medics, who informed me that I was dehydrated. I was hospitalised for two days, and was shocked to learn that one of the female staff sergeants had been making enquiries of the medics about my condition.

After I was discharged from the field hospital, I was taken off duty for two days. The same day I left the field hospital, I was summoned by the Detachment officer. He said that if I didn't change my ways and what I was doing – coming out of hospital in hat and shorts, as if I were on holiday – then he was going to put me on six months' warning, and threatened to make the commanding officer discharge me on administrative grounds. It was being suggested by them that I had been pretending to be sick.

Although I was off duty, I still had to parade. After the parade, before everybody had left for a run, the same staff sergeant had a real tirade at me at the top of her voice, saying, "What you are doing doesn't mean that you will be going home! Pretending to be sick? Not eating the food at the hospital? All you need is a kick up the rear end! You are NOT going home. It is best that you stop NOW!" she shouted. I felt that I was being picked on, especially by this staff sergeant and her close colleague. For the first time, I felt like I was being bullied; it seemed as though they wanted to target someone, to prove to their superiors their ability as competent female soldiers, who had the ambition of being promoted quickly through the ranks, and it seemed that I was being perceived by both of them to be an easy target.

I felt this was extremely unfair, to be picked on like this, especially by two other females. It seemed that my every move was being monitored very closely. In my opinion, I was no weaker than anyone else; we were in a difficult environment, and it seemed that they were determined to make my life as miserable as possible. We all had fears, which was understandable in that environment, but I was being singled out, while my White colleagues had an easy ride out there. Despite all this unwarranted scrutiny and, even though I didn't particularly want to become a clerk (as I knew my limitations), I was determined nevertheless to represent my values of hard work and determination. I was the one who had been through the pre-selection and selection processes on three separate occasions, and I was not going to allow myself to be distracted by any outward influences. This was my journey, to find my purpose in life, and to achieve the goals I had set myself, despite my personal difficulties.

I had been in Iraq for seven weeks when I was told that I would be returning home in approximately two weeks' time. This was due to the Detachment requiring clerks at home to prepare for the return of the soldiers. Shelley and I were the ones being sent home. The news that I might be returning in about two weeks' time made me very excited, as the original plan was for me to be in Iraq for three months. I was both excited and anxious. The obvious excitement was that I would be returning home, but the anxiety came from not being totally sure. Even though I was scheduled to return home, my commanders could change this at any time prior to me returning home, and delay me going. I had seen this done on several occasions to different people.

I would call Michael on average twice a day, as we could buy cards to telephone home. He was concerned that something could go wrong just when I was about to return home. We encouraged each other, and confessed our deep love for one another. We planned things we would be doing to improve our marriage, as being apart for that length of time – especially in such a potentially volatile environment – gave us the opportunity to fully appreciate each other.

The two weeks' wait to return home slowly reduced to one, and then I started counting down the days. I remained very concerned, however, that there was still the chance I could be told I would not be returning home after all, so I lived in hope that this would not be the case. The day finally came for me to return home. The journey from Camp Shaibah was pretty scary: we were driven in a minibus to Basra Airport; we all had our helmets and body armour fully in place. There were about fifteen of us on the minibus, and it was protected on all sides by a convoy of top cover sharp shooters. I must confess that I prayed from the minute the minibus left Shaibah until we were at Basra Airport. Again, we remained there until nightfall, when we were taken by plane to Kuwait. From there, we picked up the connecting flight back to the UK.

We arrived in UK airspace in the early hours of the morning; the skyline was beautiful to look at. When the pilot announced that we were within an hour of landing, there was an outburst of chattering, almost as if there were a collective sigh of relief, which was evident in the change of mood on the plane.

Coming home was really exciting. We landed at RAF Brize Norton in Oxfordshire, and it took me about an hour to gather all my stuff together. We swiftly boarded the coach bound for Warminster, and I was filled with pure joy at going home to see my wonderful husband. To say that I missed him would be a tremendous understatement. Being away had allowed me to appreciate him even more.

The coach arrived on camp just before midday. I was looking for Michael; I didn't see him in the crowd, but I knew he was there, as he had told me that he had taken a few days off to make sure he gave me the best welcome home ever. We were debriefed for a short time by the rear party commanding officer and then allowed to go home. There was a sea of people on the fringes of the parade square, waiting to welcome back their loved ones. Michael must have seen me, and approached from behind the main group of people. As I lifted my huge bag to put on my shoulder, I heard his comforting voice saying, "I'll take that," as he presented me with a single stalk of red rose, and a tender kiss on my cheek. I was a very happy woman.

7

We had two weeks' leave from work after returning from Iraq. During this time, I promptly went to see a doctor at the medical centre, as somehow I had not been feeling well since the time I'd got ill while out in Iraq. I managed to see a female civilian doctor, who was quite supportive and thorough. She took bloods and sent them to the laboratory for testing, as she said that the glands at the back of my throat were swollen, and this might indicate that my body may be fighting something. Within a week, the results of the blood test were back, and they actually confirmed that I had a virus, which I had possibly picked up when I was out in Iraq; my white blood cells were significantly higher than they should have been. The doctor prescribed antibiotics, and suggested that I take things easy and get rest and plenty of fluids. She actually put me on sick leave.

I returned to work after the end of the sick leave. I still didn't feel my usual energetic self, though, but I tried to get on with things as best I possibly could. There was talk around the office that there was a chance that I could be returning to Iraq, as there had been a change in the time soldiers were required to be out in Iraq – from three to six months. This meant that that those who were still there would remain longer than originally planned, and many of those who had come home were required to go back. The argument was that it would be cheaper to send us back than to get a new batch of soldiers trained and ready to go.

It seemed, however, that there was a direct effort from my superiors over in Iraq to get me back there. Since I was still ill, and still waiting for follow-up treatment and further tests, Cheyenne volunteered to return in my place, but they would not accept that. They then sent a request to have all three of us Jamaican girls to return out there. I went to the same female civilian doctor, who said to them that I was not currently well enough to return to a war zone, where I was expected to be at my optimum best.

The response was that I should return to Iraq to be treated and to recover. The doctor was very angry at this request, as she couldn't understand why I was being pressured to return to Iraq when it was very easy to get someone else out there, whether it was a soldier who had also returned, or one who had not been on the rear party. The doctor was quite strong in my defence, and made it clear to them that it might have been the unhygienic environment that had caused me to contract this virus; it was more feasible to get the treatment here in the UK, rather than having to go to Iraq, to a war zone which didn't have the facilities to adequately deal with this illness.

I understood that it was the female staff sergeant who was the one advocating that I return to Iraq, but her efforts were thwarted by the doctor's strong recommendation that I remain at home to receive treatment and to recover. In my view, this didn't seem to go down too well with the staff sergeant, and she was to increase her hostilities against me as retribution for not returning to Iraq.

I remained on 'rear party' (soldiers who stayed home to work at the barracks). I worked well with the other soldiers and officers to help with the efficient running of the Detachment, oftentimes working through the weekend, making sure that the fax machines were manned as well as other tasks that I was required to carry out.

The majority of personnel in the battalion returned home in late November 2004, while others returned just before Christmas. I worked over the Christmas period, as Michael and I had booked a vacation in Jamaica for the early part of January 2005. I was looking forward to this holiday so much, as this was first time I was returning home since emigrating to the UK. We planned to spend some time with our parents for the most part, but had booked a few nights in the hotel we referred to as our 'second home', Couples Ocho Rios (now known as Couples Tower Isle), which is a couples-only hotel, situated on the north east coast of the island. We spent our honeymoon there, and loved it so much that we have been back several times since, always returning to the same room, Room 304, which overlooked the beautiful Caribbean Sea. Sometimes, especially during the cold, dark winter months, when I became homesick, my therapy was to go onto their website and reminisce about the fantastic times Michael and I had there. I would picture, in my mind's eye, the chatter of the guys raking the beach of the debris that came ashore overnight, and the invigorating aroma of the coffee drifting through the breeze from the breakfast area.

I was ecstatic to return home for the first time in three years; it felt good that I was going back as a member of the British Armed Forces. This gave me a sense of accomplishment. We were met at the airport by my darling mother, who was beaming from ear to ear. I was very happy to see her; we hugged and cried together. "Yuh come back safe, mi pickney," she said, in Jamaican patois (translated this meant, "You are safely back, my child"). Our tears and sobs gradually turned into laughter. Here I was, as a visitor in my own country – this was a blessing from the Lord.

A few days into the vacation, we went to our so-called 'second home' at Couples Hotel. We were greeted at Reception with a choice of a glass of Champagne or fruit punch. We had the fruit punch, of course. Being there at Couples to me was what happiness was all about. The place hadn't changed much, but there was some erosion of the beach due to the passing of a hurricane close to the Jamaican coastline. Since it was Monday, returning guests had dinner hosted by the general manager of the hotel; all the returning guests also received a token gift. The dining room was populated mostly by American visitors, with a few Brits and the rest Canadians. Everybody was quite friendly, and shared about the number of years they had been returning to the resort, and how couples had become friends by meeting up time and again at that hotel. The conversation at our table eventually moved onto the Iraq War, and Michael mentioned that I was currently serving with the British Army and had recently done a tour of duty in Iraq. This was highlighted to the group by an elderly American gentleman and, to my utter surprise, everyone in the room gave me a standing ovation in appreciation of my service. This was extremely touching. I could hardly believe that this was actually happening to humble me; I gave Jesus all the glory.

The first full day at the hotel was quite enjoyable. We had a body massage and later lounged in the shade on the beachfront, reading a book for most of the day until it was time to get ready for dinner. That evening, we had dinner in the Italian restaurant, and after dinner we went back to our room before returning to see some of the night's entertainment. It was about half past ten when we returned to the room.

I noticed that I had a bellyache, but didn't think too much of it. As the night progressed, however, the pain intensified. I woke Michael and told him what I was experiencing, and he suggested that I watch it for the next hour to see if the pain would subside or not. Fifteen minutes later, I started vomiting uncontrollably; it was as if someone had turned a tap on. I was awash with sweat and couldn't stop vomiting. Michael rang the nurses' station, but when the nurse came, he suggested that I be taken to the St Ann Bay's Hospital, which was approximately twenty kilometres from the resort. He informed us that there was no transport on the resort to take me to the hospital, but recommended a private taxi. It was about 3.30 am when the taxi arrived. I continued vomiting in the lift going down to the taxi. I had a towel in my hand, which was full, so as soon as I arrived at the ground floor I was vomiting again, and once again in the taxi as it drove at high speed to the hospital.

We arrived at the hospital at about 3.55 am, and it didn't take too long for me to be seen by a doctor. By now, the vomiting had subsided but the doctor examined me all the same, and informed me that I would perhaps need an X-ray. However, this could not be done until after 8.00 am when the department was opened. From that time, I waited a further five hours to be seen by another doctor. He examined me and said at the top of his voice, "Your uterus is quite big; it is as if you are six months pregnant." I felt slightly offended by this comment, but did not allow it to bother me too much, as all I was concerned about was the reason for vomiting like that earlier. While on the ward, I heard the doctor talking to the nurse about me: "There is a woman with a huge uterus out there. It is as if she is six months pregnant." Again, I was disturbed at this comment, but again chose to ignore him. I was sent to have an ultrasound, which confirmed that I had at least one large fibroid, and that this was the reason for my uterus appearing enlarged. The vomiting had totally subsided by then, and I was given anti-sickness medication and told that I could go.

Michael and I left the hospital at about five in the afternoon, with my new-found friend, a girl we had met, who said that her husband lived somewhere in London. She, too, was sent home after her treatment for fibroid pain, and was driving past the resort and so offered us a lift back. We weren't sure what had caused the vomiting, but figured it might have been as a result of the mixture of food and drink that I had consumed throughout the day. We were quite disappointed that so much of our time had been spent at the hospital. Michael suggested to the nurse that he ask the general manager to extend our stay by one day to compensate for the lost time. He returned about an hour later with news that our request had been granted. We spent the extra day soaking up the ambience and the other treats that the resort offered. Apart from the illness, the time spent there was very pleasurable.

After spending a further week on the island, we reluctantly had to prepare to return to the UK. This was hard; we had just been getting used to the place again, and now had to leave to return to the cold, as well as to the added discomfort of being away from family and friends. This was our choice, however, and so we had to grit our teeth and carry on as best as possible. We arrived back in the UK on a cold but sunny January morning. I had no complaints; at least it was not grey and wet.

8

I arrived back in the UK on a Wednesday and returned to work the following day. This was a big mistake, as I honestly didn't realise how tired I was. I was physically at work, but felt so sleepy, which was evident to everyone. I had returned to work soon so that I could maximise the number of days in Jamaica on holiday, but this was a mistake and I vowed that, in future, I would come back in good time, and give myself two or three days before I returned to work. It took me a good few days to recover from the jet lag.

I went to the medical centre to see the doctor, to follow up what I had experienced in Jamaica. On this occasion, though, I saw a military doctor attached to the garrison. He asked my age, and if my husband was in the Army. I told him "No", he then asked if I was planning to start a family. I informed him that I had been trying for a family a few months after our wedding, but this was not something that we were actively pursuing at this time. He suggested that as I was getting older, it was perhaps a good time to start trying again. To be totally honest, this was the last thing I had expected: to experience a genuine care and compassion from a military doctor was quite shocking. He prescribed two months' supply of folic acid tablets. This was the first time I had actually heard about folic acid and its ability to enhance the probability of a woman conceiving. He set up another appointment for Michael and me to return to see him. Michael managed to get the time off work, and we went and saw the doctor the following week. He arranged an appointment for Michael to have a sperm count test to be done at Salisbury District Hospital.

It was a continual struggle for me, dealing with my two adversarial staff sergeants. I had made considerable effort to work with them as best as I possibly could, and at no time had I been disrespectful or insubordinate to their authority, but I was constantly being picked on by these two women. The time came for the full year appraisal, and I received a recommendation of D4, which meant 'not to be considered for promotion'. This was devastating for me, especially as I had not received the usual midyear appraisal, which informs the soldier on the performance areas in need of improvement. I was equally shocked that the Det commander and the RAO (Regimental Administrative Officer) would support this but, in my opinion, it was the staff sergeant who was running the Det. To be honest, I cried for a long time, but I called upon my inner strength to hold my head high and I resolved to carry on, despite these pressures. Michael also gave me good support. Just to encourage me, he had a bouquet of flowers delivered to me at work, which really helped. I am grateful to him also for the words of encouragement in getting me to think positively, even during the most difficult of circumstances. Being an infantry-fighting machine, the battalion was very keen on the fitness of its soldiers. Every Friday, we were required to go on the CO's run. Personally, he was very keen on his individual fitness; I guess he was leading from the front in this respect. He made it a rule that no one on the run should return after he had. Personally, I loved to run and always took up the challenge to beat the CO. I regularly ran with the guys to improve my fitness, and ran again most evenings when Michael returned home from work. One evening, Michael and I went for a run on the hills, and I ran so well that Michael could not keep up with me. In addition to the CO's run, we all had to pass the BFPA (Basic Personal Fitness Assessment), which was the Army's fitness standard. Females had to be able to run one and a half miles in under thirteen minutes (reduced from fourteen minutes), and to be able to complete twenty-one press ups and fifty sit ups in under two minutes, respectively. If this standard was not met, then the soldier was sent on a remedial fitness regime, which meant having to go to the gym at 7.00 am. Thankfully, my fitness was above average, and I was never put on the remedial fitness programme.

My friend, Cheyenne, was promoted to lance corporal, and was being posted to Germany. Shelley and I decided to organise a send-off party for her. I volunteered to do some Jamaican barbecue chicken and curried goat, instead of the usual cold sandwiches and scotched eggs. The party was on a Saturday, and I went to Bristol on the Friday to shop for the items.

I noticed that Michael and I were constantly arguing over the slightest of issues, which was unusual for us. This was a concern, as it was out of character for us to be clashing with each other like this. We usually held the view that we were in this together, and that there was strength in unity. On the day of the party, the arguing increased, and I was the instigator almost every time. I remembered that nearly everyone had been commenting on how radiant I looked, but hadn't paid any particular attention to the Combat 95s and Army boots, which did not exactly reveal a girl's true femininity. We had a reasonably good evening, but I was put off by the open comment by a female sergeant, that it would have been better if I had been a chef instead of a clerk. This hurt, as initially I didn't choose to be a clerk (as I knew my limitations). I had gone to training school anyway and had made the required standard through drive and determination. I had a right to be there, having received no favours from anyone. I hadn't received a pat on the back, nor anyone sharing any answers with me in the examinations, nor scoring my shooting to be good, when I had no clue what I had been doing at all.

Sunday came and I felt really tired, but in a different way. I wanted to sleep all the time, and I found myself craving fish and chips, which Michael went and bought for me. I went to work on Monday, and said to Cheyenne that I was feeling tired and sick, but this sickness seemed so different; I wasn't vomiting, so I didn't feel that I was pregnant. I thought that if I were pregnant, I would be vomiting, but I'd never been pregnant before. She then suggested that perhaps I could be pregnant, but I replied, "No, I've only just started that folic acid. There's no way it could have started working already." Cheyenne then replied to me, in her deep Jamaican accent, laughingly, "Nicky, that sounds like you are pregnant." She sounded quite convincing, and it finally hit home that I could indeed be pregnant.

I managed to get through the day but, as soon as Michael arrived home from work, we were down to the supermarket to buy my first pregnancy test. We were back home in a flash and then, there it was: a big bright 'plus' sign appearing on the test stick. We hugged each other, and Michael spoke softly in my ear, "Congratulations, you are going to be a great mother." I started crying, as to have my own family was a dream come true.

9

I thought to myself, 'In approximately eight months or so, I am going to be a mother.' These were exciting times in our home. Michael couldn't wipe the smile off his face, and he had an extra 'pep in his step', as they would say in Jamaica.

Deep down, though, I was reflecting on my own childhood, and the many difficulties my siblings and I had to overcome growing up in the Eleven Miles district in St Thomas, Jamaica. I had vowed that no child of mine would be born into a similar situation as I had been and, thank God, so far this has been the case.

For the most part, I could classify my childhood as traumatic and, even today, there are days when I don't want to remember some of the experiences I went through.

I was the second child for my mother, Aldith, who had five of us: Sadie, me, Teisha, George and Kimala. I was the third for my father Anthony, or 'Flanker' as he was affectionately known; he had had a daughter before he met my mother. All six children grew up in the same home, as Pamela the eldest came to live with us when she was quite young.

George, my brother, known affectionately as Dwight, was the only boy amongst five girls, and because of that he was very spoilt, especially by my dad. When he was about three years old, I can remember one Sunday morning Daddy told all of us older girls to watch him while we were all playing in the yard. There was a little tree in the front yard that he would always try to climb. I don't know what happened, as my back was turned, but all I could hear was him screaming at the top of his voice. Moments later, we realised that he had fallen out of the tree and broken his hand. Daddy went crazy, and it goes without saying that we all got a proper beating for not watching our brother.

In the early part of my childhood, as far as I can remember, things were not as bad. In fact, I can confidently say that we had a very stable happy family life. My father was employed at a nearby factory as one of the chefs, so there was a steady income. At the age of five or six, I was a happy child, and from memory my mother was also a happy housewife, who made sure that we were safe and clean, and that we had our meals at regular intervals.

My dad was my hero; he used to take us to the beach and was so playful with us, while my mother would sit on the sand, looking on and laughing. He used to take us a fair distance out, in the deep on his back, but I had full confidence in him, as he was a good swimmer from his days as a little boy, swimming in the river in Seaforth, St Thomas.

Daddy would also take us mango picking in the hills (mango bush) at the border of St Andrew and St Thomas in Jamaica. At times, we walked far distances, as far as seven to eight miles approximately. When we were too tired to walk, he would carry us on his back, and each of us would get the chance to have that comfort.

Also, my dad and his friends would go crab hunting during the rainy season, and there was a lot of excitement when they returned home, the crabs were put inside the huge boiling pot filled with all sorts of seasoning and whole corn. Approximately fifteen minutes to half an hour later all of us children would be busy cracking the crab's legs searching for the meat within, very determined to get out as much as possible despite being exasperated by the fumes of scotched bonnet pepper.

When Daddy cooked at home, that was the best. He used up everything, though, cooking two or three different meats for dinner; he served breakfast as if he were at work. It was plentiful and nice – very different from my mother's cooking. Whenever he was in the kitchen, my mum was barred, and there was a great atmosphere of childlike bantering. Mummy and all of us children were so very happy.

The factory where he was employed started to make the workers redundant. This affected the economy of the community, which also caused a high level of anxiety in the neighbourhood, as many people depended on this factory for employment to support their families. My father, as far as I can remember, made the decision to leave this job before he was made redundant. I guess he jumped before he was pushed.

This had a big impact on us, as this income no longer existed. At that point in time, my dad was approximately twenty-eight or twenty-nine years old. Having six young children and a wife to provide for, he went in search of other jobs on a daily basis – to no avail. He, however, used his initiative, and set up a cook shop on St Thomas' main road, just outside our home. This venture was successful at times, but was not viable in the long term. He started buying the meat and other supplies on credit, but was not able to pay the creditors on time, which impacted on his credibility and respectability. I have no doubt that this contributed to a number of arguments that he and my mother would have, as many people would turn up asking for payment for their goods, and she was the one who had to face them most of the time.

He had no option but to close this little business down. While he was working as a chef at the factory, he cooked at a number of Christmas and dinner parties for the owners and their friends, and built up a good reputation – especially as an excellent seafood chef. He used these contacts to get another job, this time at the popular Sea Witch Restaurant in New Kingston. This was a welcome relief for all of us children; there was hope again that our lives would return to normal. Things got better for a while, as he was now earning a reasonable salary from this establishment.

Not long after taking the job at Sea Witch Restaurant, there was a marked change in my dad's behaviour. I can remember he would not come home after work in the evenings; his excuse was that he was working late. My mum would ask him where he'd slept and he told her that he'd slept at work. Deep down, Mummy knew that he was lying. This escalated from not coming home at nights, to extended periods of one or two weeks at a time, and up to a month or even two on occasions. This was truly disturbing for me, as our family life deteriorated quite rapidly and significantly. We had little or no food; my mum tried her hardest to feed the family, but only had enough food to eat two times for the day.

My mother did a subsistence job, selling the informal Chinese number-gambling game commonly known in Jamaica as 'drop pan'. However, for some reason, this little job didn't last for too long and, for the most part, we had no money coming in, apart from what her sisters in Canada, especially Aunty Muriel, would occasionally send to her. Aunty Muriel was like a mother to my mum.

When my father stopped coming home, he would send messages for us to come by his workplace for money. Sometimes it was a waste of time to turn up there, as he would come up with all sorts of excuses why he didn't have any money to give to us. While this was happening, my education suffered tremendously, because my mother now had to be making survival decisions about whether we should go to school or have food to eat, and even then we still didn't have food.

When she had money, my mother bought her shopping from a lady known as Miss Linnette, who had a shop in the village. When things got harsher for us financially, in order to feed us my mother would send me to Miss Linnette to get some food on credit. As young as I was, I felt a deep sense of shame that we had to do this, but I had to go in order for us to have food.

I was the only child of my siblings, who was willing to go with the little note with the list of items that she wanted on credit. I guess my mother herself was embarrassed, and that was the reason that she herself didn't go either; this was left to me.

There were times when Miss Linnette seemed frustrated and impatient with us, but at no time did she refuse to send what was requested by my mother, as she knew that she would eventually get paid. I've remembered this all my life, and wish to thank her for her understanding and support as, without her, I don't know how we would have survived.

Whatever my father was doing, whether he had another woman or his actions were due to gambling, it had a significantly negative impact on all of our lives. The man I had grown to love and respect – and even feared and adored – gambled with our futures, which left me significantly scarred. It was not that he hadn't been working – he was gainfully employed in a reasonably good job – it was that he chose to abandon us at that critical stage of our development.

We lived on the St Thomas main road. I can remember us standing at the gate, desperately looking for him to come off the bus, especially when we were so hungry. On a couple of occasions in the past, he would eventually come home, and it would be as if it were Christmas for us; he would arrive with bags and bags of groceries, those large brown paper shopping bags. It would take a long time for him to get them all off the bus. Whenever this happened, I would be very happy and it would seem as if all my troubles would be taken away. My mother, still a young woman, would be so happy, despite desperately missing him and having to face the cries of hunger from the children on her own. She would welcome him with a naïve love, which seemed almost unconditional.

There were periods when he would be home for up to three months, but still went missing several nights during the week. I sensed that he would be on edge, itching to get away. I can remember that was when the arguments started; he began to accuse my mother of having extramarital affairs – a claim which was totally unfounded. We lived in a small two-bedroom house and neighbours could hear the arguments; my mother defending herself and crying, while rejecting these cruel accusations. It seemed as though he was using reverse psychology as a control mechanism on my poor mother.

I was so shaken by the entire ordeal. I would be so nervous and frightened that my hands would literally shake with fear. I couldn't take the shouting and swearing and threatening from my dad. I thought that he would hit my mum, and this fear became reality one night, when I was about nine years old. They had started to fight. My dad is well over six feet tall with a muscular frame, and my mother markedly shorter; she was no match for him physically. I remember running in between them, crying, as I didn't want him to kill her. I cried, "No, Daddy, no Daddy, don't kill Mummy." I was the only child of my siblings who cried and begged Daddy not to hit Mum. I felt ashamed to be seen in daylight, as all the neighbours would be aware that my parents had been arguing and fighting.

Even when I went to school, I would still be traumatised, as I would spend quite a lot of time thinking that he would hurt her, especially if I knew that he hadn't gone to work. This also contributed to a lack of concentration on my schoolwork, even though we didn't go to school regularly.

I loved school so much, despite the struggle to attend. I never attended during the first week of term, as my mother would say that nothing important happens during the first week. I thought, however, that this was her defence at not being able to send us due to lack of money. My father would often go missing during this critical time. By the time I got to school the second week, I had to sit at the back of the class, as all the other students had taken the best seats. As a result, it would take me a while to settle in and make friends. Because I'd taken breaks from school, the teachers didn't pay much attention to me either; I didn't blame them, as I hadn't been there.

I can remember that things got so bad for us financially that I was not able to go to school. In my desperation, though, I would say to my mother that she could give me the bus fare, and I would get lunch on credit from Jasmine, one of the ladies who sold at the school gate. In appreciation for what Jasmine did, I showed loyalty by only buying from her whenever we had money. These were my primary school years, and life was a struggle just to get a basic education.

This lack of attendance at school meant that I would always be in the slowest stream, which was very humiliating for me. This affected me psychologically, and sometimes I would just burst into tears while sitting in class. I felt that both my parents had badly let me down in not ensuring that I received a basic primary school education.

I attended St Benedict's Primary School, which was located almost directly on the border of two communities of Harbour View and Bull Bay, in the parish of St Andrew, Jamaica. It was a Catholic institution. The fact that I was in the slower stream meant that our class was always the last group to leave or enter the church after devotions or other functions we attended there, and the ones who sat at the back of the building as we got to the more senior grades. When I was younger, there was a part of the church that I deemed to be special, as only the bright children in the early years would sit there. I had always wanted to be able to sit there but was not allowed to, but one day, when the public health nurses came in to administer vaccinations, I finally had the grand opportunity to sit there. I can see myself now; I sat in every seat, bouncing on each one as I went around. This felt so good, no other groups were in the church at the time, and finally this was my chance to sit in the chairs normally reserved for the brighter classes, especially in the early years. I thought I deserved the chance to be amongst the brightest children, but had been failed by my parents.

Despite the many difficulties that I had faced as a child: struggling to go to school regularly to achieve an education – especially in the early years; the difficulties of not having any food to eat, and the trauma that this brought, as I grew older I was determined to make the most of any opportunities that came my way, so that any prospective children would receive a much better quality of life than I had received. Now that I was pregnant with our first child, this had become a reality, and I was happy that with the help of Jesus Christ and the support of a very caring and hardworking husband, together we would make this possible.

10

The next day, I made an appointment to see the doctor at the medical centre, and he confirmed that I was approximately six weeks pregnant. He issued me a medical downgrade form. This form clearly stated the conditions under which I could carry out my duties, and what I could and should not do. I was required to give a copy to my immediate managers.

I went back to work and gave one of the seniors – the same female sergeant – the form. She knew immediately what it was, and said, "Congratulations," and seemed quite civil. She then asked how was I feeling, and I told her that I wasn't feeling too well. She suggested, however, that she would accompany me to take the form to the staff sergeant. As we approached her office, she was coming down the corridor from the direction of the RAO's office.

We met her at her office door, and the sergeant said, "Private Hall is pregnant and she is not feeling too well." The staff sergeant snatched the paper from me and said, "Do you think that this means you will be going off sick?" I had not gone there to say that I wanted to go on sick leave; they had asked me a question about how I was feeling and I had given an honest response, yet the staff sergeant was behaving as if I had requested time off from work. I had no intention of going off work; I was in the early stages of pregnancy for the first time and wasn't feeling well, and this woman had started to abuse me. There I was, a twenty-nine-year-old married woman, being treated as a child.

"Wait here," she said angrily. "I will have to take this to the RAO." She came back after taking copies of the form, and I returned to doing my job. The despicable treatment by this staff sergeant was to deteriorate to a new low. Ever since they knew of my pregnancy, it was as if I was being penalised for being pregnant.

A couple of days later, I was called by the same staff sergeant to go and see her in her office. She said, "I hope you won't be letting the side down by going off sick. From my experience, in the early days whenever a woman got pregnant, she had to leave the Army. I am not saying that you are going to go off sick all the time, but I am just saying this to you." She continued, "Many times I have called other girls in the Det into the office and have told them things, and they haven't repeated it, so don't tell anybody about this conversation." I honestly couldn't believe what I was hearing from this woman. 'This is sexual discrimination and intimidation – from a woman at that,' I thought to myself, and she was covering this up by keeping me from telling anyone else about this. I was taken aback and utterly shocked by what I'd heard. In fact, I couldn't even begin to believe what I was hearing.

During this time, the Detachment was preparing for the regimental inspection by the inspection team from the Adjutant General's Corps. Even though I wasn't feeling well, I worked really hard to contribute to the Det's success in passing the inspection. We worked till late every evening, sometimes up to 9.00 pm. We were required to go into work at the weekend. I didn't have a problem with that, as in the Army you were paid for every day, so they could order you to work on any weekend. I went into work over the weekend, and this was to prove to be very costly for me, as I ended up getting chicken pox for the first time – aged twenty-nine.

I strongly believe that I caught the chicken pox from a colleague, who had been forced to go into work with her one-year-old child, who had been infected with the chicken pox at the time. From what I gathered, she had explained to the bosses that her child was infected with chicken pox and that she couldn't get anyone to look after him. In addition, her husband (who was also serving with the regiment) was away for the weekend, on a training exercise on Salisbury Plain. The bosses told her that if she couldn't find a minder for the baby then she would have to bring him into the office with her.

Just a couple days later, I started really feeling ill. I had a sore throat and a constant headache that refused to go away. I wanted to go to see the doctor, but was reluctant to do so because I didn't want to be seen to be 'letting the side down'. When several areas of my head started to itch, and I saw a couple of tiny bumps in my face, however, I immediately went to see the doctor. On this occasion, I saw a young Army doctor, who seemed genuinely concerned about the diagnosis of chicken pox. He informed me of the potential dangers that this disease could have to the unborn child and to me. He was on the phone straightaway to his boss, a colonel who also worked at the medical centre. He then made a number of phone calls to consultants in Bristol and Southampton, who were experts in the field of virology, regarding how best to deal with this situation. He informed me that there was an eighty percent chance that, since I had contracted chicken pox in the early stages of pregnancy, my child could be deformed with limbs and other organs not developing properly, as well as blindness.

I was absolutely devastated and frightened at the prospect that my child could be born deformed or blind as a result of me contracting chicken pox. This was a lot to go through, with Michael as my only support.

While all this was happening, the consultant at Salisbury District Hospital confirmed that I had at least one uterine fibroid, which also posed a potential risk to the baby as he or she grew within the womb. I could hardly believe that all this was happening to me. I had no idea that pregnancy could bring so many worries.

The doctors at the medical centre gave me a considerable amount of care in order to monitor the baby and me. They gave me two appointments per week to ensure that the baby was growing properly, and to monitor the pain that I had started having with the fibroid. The hospital was also concerned with the presence of the fibroid, and gave me two appointments per month so they could monitor the growth of the baby and the fibroid.

There was immense pressure from the people at work, however. They kept questioning why I needed to go to the medical centre twice a week. There was no care about what was happening to me; there was no sympathy whatsoever, in fact. I informed the Detachment commander, of every piece of information that I received from both the medical centre and the hospital, so they were fully aware of the difficulties that I was experiencing. Still, however, they put me under immense pressure, which compounded my worries.

By the end of June 2005, I was approximately three months pregnant. Michael and I went to the St Paul's carnival in Bristol. Going to the carnival, for us, was a way of soaking up some our Jamaican culture, which we missed. It wasn't carnival as in the Caribbean; we went to buy sugar cane, jerk chicken and some curried goat, and probably saw people we wouldn't see in rural Wiltshire.

We parked our car near to the area where the carnival was taking place. However, I noticed that I was experiencing severe cramps in my lower abdomen and could hardly walk. The more I walked the more severe and unbearable the pain became. We spent about an hour getting the food and taking a look around before I decided to return home. I had to be taking tiny steps because of the excruciating pain. This further added to my frustration; I knew I wasn't weak and was normally fit and well but, so far, pregnancy was proving very difficult for me.

According to the consultant at Salisbury District Hospital, even though I was around three months pregnant, my stomach was the size of a woman who was five or six months pregnant, due to the size of the fibroid. At one of the consultations, it was confirmed that the fibroid was the size of a small grapefruit, but the good thing was that it was on the outside of the womb, which gave some hope that the baby could still survive. He explained to me that the fibroid might be degenerating, because the blood supply was now diverting to nourish the baby. This is what had been causing the excruciating pain at times.

The fear about the chicken pox affecting the health of the baby still existed. The consultants had suggested that, due to the high probability that the baby could be deformed, I should consider having an abortion. I discussed this option with Michael, and came to the conclusion that I would give my child the best chance to live. After all, this was only a possibility, and the doctors were still not totally sure it would affect the baby.

They had also planned for us to have an amniocentesis done. This is a procedure where a test is carried out to diagnose whether or not the baby has developed any abnormalities. The procedure involved putting a needle near my naval to withdraw fluids that would be tested for abnormal chromosomes. We explored this procedure but, having been told about the likelihood that this could trigger a miscarriage, we decided against doing it, and prayed and depended on God to take care of this whole situation, as He knows all things.

11

I honestly do not know why this female staff sergeant hated me so much. On one occasion, I was the duty clerk, which meant that I would be the personnel who manned the Regimental Head Office until the last officer left for the day, and would go in early the next day to ensure the building was opened.

That day, the Det was going on a walk to a pub. The staff sergeant said that she wanted me to go on the walk as well. Considering that I was the duty clerk – and also having a difficult pregnancy – I decided that I would stay behind, like my two other pregnant colleagues. She still enquired if I was going and I answered, "No, Staff, I will stay behind and do some work." She then replied, "The other two are doing something for their sergeant major," and then left the room. I felt bemused and saddened at what was happening; there were three of us who were pregnant, yet I was the only one being pressured to take this walk to a pub. A few moments later, she returned and said in an angry tone, "The Det commander wants you to be there." I couldn't fight it anymore. I cried, as I couldn't understand why the other two were being allowed to remain behind. I guess my baby was less valuable than theirs.

We weren't driving to this pub, nor was it a short stroll; it was a cross-country trek, which involved walking on paths and roads over several hills. Considering that I was over sixteen weeks pregnant; all the difficulties I had been experiencing to date;

the pain and stiffness in my belly whenever I walked long distances, no one seemed to care about my welfare and that of my child. This was my reality, though, and I had to fight on, without appearing to be insubordinate to the higher-ranking officers. I tried my best to stand my ground, but was forced to go on the walk.

Shelley and I set out to go to this pub. Approximately two kilometres into this walk, I felt really tired and my belly became very stiff. I felt a piercing sensation in my abdomen, so I mentioned how I was feeling to Shelley. She used some very choice words and said, "No, Nicky, you cannot do this." She told me to wait where I was, and she would go back to camp and get her car. We had to drive a good distance to get to this pub on the outskirts of Warminster. The irony was that, after taking me off clerk duty and forcing me to go on this walk while sixteen weeks pregnant, both the Det commander and the staff sergeant turned up, but they drove. I didn't have a problem going to the pub; my issue was that they wanted me to walk such a long distance in the state I was in. When I returned to the office, I resumed my role as duty clerk.

One of the clerks, a corporal at the time, was also upset that I had allowed them to force me to go on this walk, while the other two sat on their backsides in the office. I told her that I had tried my hardest to stand up for myself but, as a private soldier, I did not stand a chance against a captain and a staff sergeant without appearing insubordinate. I tried my best not to focus on these people too much, but to put my energies into protecting this baby growing inside me as much as possible.

A couple of weeks later, I received a letter for a twenty-week scan at the Salisbury District Hospital.

This was scheduled for August 2, 2005. We already knew that we were having a girl, as we had had regular scans at the hospital. We decided to call her Hope. Michael thought it was a good name, especially due to the difficulties that I was experiencing with the pregnancy.

The doctors still had concerns that the baby could be deformed, but the twenty-week scan would give some idea about what was happening with regards to her growth, etc.

The pain from the fibroid was debilitating at times, so much so that I could not move and just had to lie in bed. It often felt as though the baby was squashing the fibroid or vice versa. The consultant had warned us that, because of the size of the fibroid, there was a high probability of miscarriage or at least not going to full term. I believe the plan was to try to get the pregnancy to around thirty weeks' gestation, but for me this was a struggle, as the pain seemed to increase daily and the only pain relief was paracetamol.

To be treated this way at work was difficult for me to take. As far as I knew, the other two were not being treated in the same way, and they were having far easier pregnancies. At no time did any of my supervisors ask how I was coping, or even how the appointments had been going.

Friday, July 29, 2005 was to be forever etched in my memory. I had been feeling ill all day, having had intense abdominal cramps for most of the day. When Michael arrived home, I asked him to ring the hospital at around 5.30 pm. They told him to take me to Wilton Ward that same evening, and the duty registrar would check me over. Wilton Ward was a gynaecological ward. I had been placed on this ward and not on an antenatal ward because the pregnancy was less than the twenty-four weeks threshold that the hospital deemed that the pregnancy was viable. At least, that was what we were told.

I arrived on the ward at around half past eleven and was given a bed. It took about half an hour to see the registrar, who did the checks and decided that I would be admitted to monitor the baby and to try to control the pain. The consultant had informed us earlier that my pregnancy was deemed to be high risk, and made the provision that I could call into the ward whenever I was struggling with the pain from the fibroid or feeling generally unwell.

The first night in the hospital was fairly straightforward: they administered pain relief and did regular checks on the baby. I felt that being in hospital in the care of the medics meant that my baby would be safe. How wrong did this notion prove to be! The pain just increased and became unbearable. I believe that my pain threshold is quite high, but when the pain came on, it was like nothing I had felt before.

On Sunday, a doctor told me that they would be discharging me that day, as there was nothing more they could do to reduce the pain I was feeling. She suggested that it was better for me to go home to deal with the pain in a different way, such as acupuncture, aromatherapy and other forms of relaxation, to take my mind off the pain. There was nothing else the staff could do because the fibroid appeared to be degenerating, and that was what was causing the pain. I was shocked that I was in so much pain yet they were sending me home. I was afraid that if I went home, the pain would cause me to go into premature labour, and being in the hospital would prevent this. Maybe I was being quite naïve but, with all the emotion that I was going through, I thought that was the most logical position to take.

They decided to let me stay in hospital but wanted to put me at the back of the ward. I requested that my bed not be moved. This was eventually agreed to but, in my opinion, I noticed a deterioration in the level of care I received. Meanwhile, the pain remained constant. Michael had taken a couple of days off work, in order to support me. We didn't have any other support, apart from maybe our friends from church, but the distance from Bristol made it unlikely that they would travel all the way down to Salisbury.

Monday, I was still in a lot of pain. Whatever they gave just was not effective in reducing or removing the pain. The concoction of pain relief included pethidine, dihydrocodeine and paracetamol. It was a difficult and delicate balancing act, trying to control the pain while trying to protect the baby at the same time. Understandably, the doctors were more concerned about the baby than they were about me.

I felt, though, that I was being neglected by the nursing staff. Michael came to visit me in hospital at about 7.00 am. He gave me a wash, and was there to give me a shoulder to lean on. I made several trips to the toilet, crying in anguish, and absolutely no one offered any support or even a word of comfort. I asked for more pain relief, and was given another cocktail, which included oramorph (a liquid form of morphine, which is one of the strongest forms of pain relief).

I spoke to one of the senior nurses, and told her that I'd had no previous experience in giving birth, but the pain became more severe in five-minute intervals, and they felt like contractions. A doctor then came and had a listen to my bowels, and said that it sounded fine. Maybe I was constipated as a result of the amount of medication I had been taking. She prescribed fybogel – a medicine that helps to relieve constipation. No mention was made about the baby at this stage.

I was still languishing in pain for a fair while longer. Michael asked a nurse to have my blood pressure reading taken; this was done by a student nurse, who confirmed that it was high. The pain and the contractions started to increase, and became even more unbearable. Again, they gave me oramorph, which didn't help. A nurse came and told me to go for a walk and try to take my mind off the pain. I walked out of Wilton ward down the corridor, but had to return to the ward hastily as the pain intensified. I requested more pethidine but they refused, because they said it was very addictive, so they offered the gas and air, which helped to alleviate the pain. I walked along the corridor, wheeling the cylinder and taking puffs when the pain became unbearable. At one point, I mentioned to Michael that gas and air were normally given to a woman who was actually in labour, but I didn't think anything more about it. I suddenly felt like I needed the toilet, but thought it was the fybogel starting to work. I told Michael, and he accompanied me. We took the gas and air cylinder to the toilet with us, in case the pain returned, but very soon after I felt a relief, as if I wanted to pass faeces. Instead of passing faeces, however, I felt the pressure coming from the front. I told Michael that it was not coming from the back, but from the front. I put my hand down there to feel what was happening. I felt a hard object. By this time, my mind was running very fast, and I thought to myself, "My baby." I screamed loudly, and said to Michael, "The baby is coming!" My instinct was to try to push the baby back up, but obviously it was far too late for that. I felt a sudden painful headache, "Michael, it is the baby," I said, in a loud and frantic voice. I then heard my husband cry out a loud wail in anguish. We were in one of the bathrooms at the time, and it seemed as if his voice reverberated across to some of the other wards.

Minutes later, there we were, surrounded by several doctors and nurses. I had actually been in labour all this time, and none of the medical professionals had known, or had they? I was in a state of shock. I just could not believe what was happening to me. A female registrar took charge of all the medics around us. She was very matter-of-fact, and stated that she saw a membrane. There was nothing they could have done to save our baby; it seemed that it was the fibroid which caused the miscarriage. This may well have been the case, but the medical care I received was poor. In my opinion, I had been treated worse than if I had been in a government hospital in a third world country.

I told them that I felt as if I still needed to pass faeces, and was told to sit on a commode, and if I needed to pass faeces I should go ahead. To me, this was quite appalling; it was clear that I was in the middle of a miscarriage, yet they still wanted me to suffer the indignity of giving birth to our dead baby on a nasty commode. I told them that if I was going to pass faeces then I would do it on a bed, because I didn't want our baby to be born in commode.

The worst day of my life so far only got worse. I was then told that I would have to give birth to my dead baby. They attached a couple of drips to me, and led me to a side room, where I had to push the baby out of me. I was utterly devastated, but held my composure as best I could. Hope was now dead, and I wanted to preserve my own life. They pulled the baby out of me, "She is beautiful," Michael said, and he started wailing again. I had to lie there for a further two hours while the placenta and foetal membranes came out. A midwife wrapped her up and handed her to me; I fixed my eyes on her and just cried and cried. No sound came out of me – I was just so numb – only rivers and rivers of tears.

They gave us a room on the delivery suite to recover. I was given painkillers and antibiotics. The sister on shift that evening told us that it was important that we took pictures of the baby, as this would form part of our memory. She also took her footprints and palm prints that she suggested would form part of our memoirs. I don't know if either Michael or I slept, but I can remember Michael reassuring me that I had done nothing wrong, that he was very proud of me, and someday I was going to be a great mother. God will bless us again, and only the Lord knew why this had happened to us. We had named our baby Hope; she was now dead. My first ever child was dead but, because of the Christ in me, I had not lost hope, the hope that one day I would be a mother and have a beautiful family.

At about 7.30 the next morning, Michael went to have a meeting with the sister in charge of Wilton ward, and left me on my own in the room we had stayed in overnight. Michael had only been gone for approximately five minutes when I took the baby tenderly in my arms and began walking up the corridor, sobbing and shaking her from side to side repeating, "My baby! My baby!" It was a cleaner who saw me, and raised the alarm that a woman, looking very wild and in a poor mental state, was walking along the corridor with a dead baby.

A chaplain came and took the baby from me, and tried to calm me down. He assured me that they would look after her caringly and respectfully. I was hurting at this stage, and felt that I had failed my child and my husband. I started to blame myself for this tragedy that had happened to us. I thought to myself that if I had been able to go home when they said they were going to discharge me, then I would not have lost my baby.

I felt a deep sense of shame that, just a couple of days before, I was pregnant with my baby, who was expected to be born in December, and now she was no more. Many people, who knew that I was pregnant, would be curious to know what had happened, and I didn't have the strength to face all the questions.

I felt that I had given them the opportunity to mistreat me, which had resulted in the death of my baby. How could I have been in labour, even given all sorts of pain relief, including gas and air, and none of the medical professionals were aware that I was in labour? I was twenty weeks pregnant, not having any previous experience of childbirth, and had gone to the Salisbury District Hospital to protect my baby, but instead lost my precious child there, in my opinion, under extraordinary circumstances of negligence and maltreatment.

12

After spending twenty-four hours on the maternity ward, I was discharged on Wednesday, August 3, 2005. I was very surprised that, after being seen by the consultant, I was sent home with no antibiotic medication nor a scan done to ensure that there were no retained products left inside of me.

I hadn't been home one full hour, when I told Michael that I was experiencing quite a lot of pain. Michael rushed me immediately back to the hospital. We returned to the maternity ward at about 5.00 pm, and were seen by a senior registrar. Michael insisted that I had a scan, and the doctor arranged for one to be done the following day. He arranged for me to remain in hospital overnight, and I had the scan on Thursday. The radiologist informed us that he could see some retained products inside me, but the consultant obstetrician stated, however, that he was comfortable in sending me home with painkillers – but he still refused to prescribe any antibiotics.

The next day, I started feeling severe abdominal and back pains and had a high fever. Michael rang the community midwife at the Frome hospital, and he was advised to ring 999 for an ambulance. When the ambulance team came, they were very alarmed that my blood pressure and temperature were elevated – especially since I had recently had a miscarriage. I was taken to the Salisbury District Hospital once again.

I was taken to Accident and Emergency, and was referred to the obstetrician/gynaecologist on duty – the same doctor from the day before – who said that I was to be admitted to Wilton ward. You can imagine that I did not want to see that ward again, nor the same people who worked on it who, I felt, had failed in their duty of care to me. She gave me the option of going home, stating that all she would be administering to me would be painkillers and antibiotics, and this I could do at home. I left A&E at about 4.00 am on Saturday, August 6. Because we had taken the ambulance down to the hospital we didn't have the car, so we had to call a cab home to Warminster. The fare was not cheap but the cab driver knocked off £10 so we only paid £40. I just wanted to go home to try to understand what was happening to me.

The turmoil surrounding the loss of my baby and the subsequent health concerns only got progressively worse. On Sunday, August 7, I went to use the toilet. To my surprise, I felt something fell from inside me, and heard a loud splash in the toilet bowl. I had a quick look and shouted hysterically: "Michael! Something fell out of me into the toilet!"

"Where?" he asked.

"There," I replied, pointing into the toilet. He quickly got a pair of medical gloves from a broken box he had he taken home from work.

On examination, the object looked like a piece of placenta that had remained inside of me. I was very frightened to say the least, and concerned that this might have become septic, and that the subsequent infection could have killed me.

The community midwife turned up within five minutes of this occurring to do her follow-up visit. Michael showed her a picture of the object that fell from inside of me. She showed some concern, and rang the Salisbury District Hospital immediately. She spoke to a senior registrar. He arranged for me to have another scan at the obstetrics and gynaecology outpatient ward.

I went on Monday and had the scan done. The radiographer appeared uncomfortable at what she had seen. I was subsequently seen by a junior doctor, who admitted that she was unable to interpret what the radiographer had put into the report. We also told her that we had a friend who is a General Practitioner, who advised us to demand a D&C (a surgical procedure performed following miscarriage). The junior doctor said that she was not able to answer our concerns but would relay our concerns to the consultant.

He came to see us and we requested to have the D&C. He stated that the D&C was unnecessary because that piece of placenta was probably the final piece, and he would hopefully not need to see me again until the consultation in six to eight weeks' time. I was disappointed that he was rather dismissive of our D&C request, especially considering all I had been through with the miscarriage and the placenta falling out of me. I honestly thought the consultant would have given me due care and attention to ensure nothing else would go wrong and that I wouldn't have to suffer any more at the hands of the hospital staff, who I felt had failed me since I was first admitted on July 31.

I left hospital again on Monday, August 8, 2005, very disturbed that these people were still not listening to us. Not only was I dealing with the emotions of losing my first child, but I was also fighting to stay alive. Approximately a week after the consultation with the consultant, I was fearful of contracting a life- threatening infection. This was a worry, as I had a serious allergy to penicillin, and so the medics would need to be very skilful in prescribing me with antibiotics.

On Tuesday, August 16, 2005, the day following the burial of our baby, I went to the bathroom at about 6.00 am to use the toilet again and, once again, pieces of placenta, measuring about 4 cm in diameter, fell from me into the toilet bowl. About three minutes later, while standing at the bathroom door, yet another piece – this one measuring about 4.5 cm in diameter – forced itself out of me. I screamed, "Michael, what is happening to me?" Michael, still a bit sleepy, rushed to support me when he saw the pieces of placenta falling from within me. I was dumbfounded that, having lost our baby and literally having to plead to have a D&C done, two weeks after the miscarriage, retained membrane was still falling from me. What had I done to deserve this absolutely despicable treatment?

Again, Michael rang the community midwife at Frome Hospital, who again advised him to ring 999 for an ambulance. Instead, he rang Wilton ward at Salisbury District Hospital. He spoke to a nurse who told him to bring me in immediately. When I arrived at the hospital, I was examined by a registrar, who immediately organised for the D&C procedure to be done. The surgery was done at about 3.00 pm on Tuesday. The doctor who performed the surgery informed Michael that she had to remove even more bits of placenta. All this could have become septic and killed me. I am grateful to God, who kept me alive through this terrible ordeal. My contact with Salisbury District Hospital was a regrettable one, and I vowed never to return to that institution again.

13

The hospital wanted to have Hope's body cremated almost immediately, but Michael and I requested that a post mortem be done, so that we could find out why did our baby died. We also wanted to know if the baby would have been affected as result of my contracting chicken pox in the very early stages of pregnancy.

We also decided that we wanted to have a funeral to serve as a point of closure for us. This had been a particularly devastating event in our lives, and so a funeral would allow us to have a place to go back to whenever we felt like, and would serve as a place we could take any future children to visit, to show where their sibling was buried.

The consultant and his team were insistent that it was the fibroid that had caused me to miscarry. I disagree, and am almost certain that, had I received more care and attention, then my baby would have survived.

The sad thing is the results of the post mortem revealed that Hope would have been perfectly normal.

Planning Hope's funeral was very difficult for us; we didn't have anyone we considered to be close family to support us during that time and, in addition, I had to go in and out of hospital on several occasions.

We owe a great debt of gratitude to our friends, Sonia Carr, who took it upon herself to totally organise every aspect of the funeral, thus allowing us to start to grieve for our baby, and Yvonne Bailey and her family, who came round with dinner almost every evening in an attempt to ensure that Michael and I were eating.

On the morning of August 15, 2005, I got out of bed at about 6.30 am feeling numb. Up to that time, the reality of what had taken place hadn't really hit home. I was still in shock and disbelief that, instead of expecting to be taking my baby home in a couple of months' time, I was preparing to attend her funeral. Most people would never know how it feels to bury your own child, but I can assure you that it is definitely not the natural thing to have to do.

I can remember that, even two weeks after losing the baby, I subconsciously believed that I was still pregnant; that the due date was the end of December, and that my pregnancy hormones were still running very high. It was as though I was still protective of this thing that was no longer there. During pregnancy, I had always made sure that if I had eggs they were well done. I wept uncontrollably the first time I realised I was still having my eggs well done, even though she was no longer with us. I had never cried like this before now, but this was a good old cry. I felt a lot better.

The funeral took place at a cemetery in the City of Bath, in the south west of England. It was attended by Sonia and a few other close friends, who did their best to distract us from our pain. The Army chaplain came up from Blandford in Dorset, and Reverend Raymond Veira the pastor of the church in Bristol that we attended also came to support us. I am not sure why the chaplain from the 1 Black Watch did not attend, and neither did anyone from the Welfare department of 1 Black Watch attend. My colleagues from the Adjutant General's Corps Detachment, for which I worked in Warminster, also failed to come and support us. This was truly disappointing, as the Army is usually regarded as an 'extended family' that normally takes care of its own. In my time of bereavement, however, I felt that I was left on my own: having experienced such a tragic loss, we were not supported by this 'family'. Even the Chaplain expressed shock that none of them had attended, despite both the Welfare department and the senior managers in the Detachment having had full knowledge of the date and time.

A couple of days after the funeral, the regimental administrative officer made a visit to our home, with what seemed to be a humane proposal. He suggested that, since there were two other females in the office, whose pregnancies were still progressing, he was prepared to have me posted to a new regiment on what is known as a compassionate posting away from Warminster, so that I wouldn't be affected by having to see them. I thought that this was a good idea, and took some time to consider this. But, while this seemed like a reasonable option to consider, I began to notice that I was becoming more tearful and anxious. On one occasion, the anxiety was so bad that I became hysterical and short of breath. Poor Michael didn't know what to do, so he rang Frome Maternity Unit once again. The midwife then informed me that I was having a panic attack; this was normal due to the sustained, traumatic experiences I had recently experienced. These panic attacks would subside after blowing into a brown paper bag.

I started to develop severe, persistent headaches, which hurt in a way that I had never experienced before. The pain was primarily concentrated to the left frontal region of my head and, at times, I had excruciating toothache mostly on the left side of my mouth.

The first doctor I saw after the miscarriage was a female doctor, whose husband was also an Army doctor. I was like a special case to them. The minute I stepped inside the facility and spoke to the receptionist, I was made to feel special.

The doctor came for me at Reception. "Hello, Necola. Please come through," she said respectfully.

"Hi, Ma'am," I replied, walking with my head held high. I was quite conscious that all my mannerisms were being observed.

"You look radiant today, Necola, considering all you have been through," she continued.

"Thank you," I replied, in appreciation of the compliment and smiled. Part of the reason why I smiled was that, on Michael's recommendation, I had gone to get my hair cut low a few days earlier, in what most Black women would know as the Toni Baxter hairstyle. I had on a lime green cotton top, with a flowing ankle length white skirt and a flat pair of leather sandals. I was trying very hard to be positive, despite losing my child under the circumstances I had, and the subsequent ordeal of potentially dying from septic shock.

I described the headache symptoms to the doctor, and she immediately expressed concern that I may be entering the early stages of postnatal depression; the perceived pains were symptomatic of the onset of such a condition. She went on to share that she, too, had experienced multiple miscarriages, and had been on anti-depression medication herself.

She explained that there was a potential chemical imbalance in the brain, due to the shock of losing the baby and the other, subsequent health concerns, so I should go away and think about starting medication. I said that I would pray about it and let her know my decision.

Growing up in Jamaica, I had not heard of postnatal depression before. The first time you ever discovered that someone was suffering from mental health problems was when you saw them walking insanely on the streets. There was also a distinctly negative stigma towards people who suffered with mental health issues, and I did not want to be identified in such a category. My main dilemma, however, was as a born again Christian, how was I to deal with the problem of suffering from postnatal depression? I was not prepared to accept this.

I feared that the severe pains I had been feeling on the left side of my brain were due to a brain tumour – at least that was what my mind was telling me. The doctor arranged a dental appointment to investigate what was causing the excruciating toothache. I attended this appointment along with Michael and my mother, who had arrived a couple days earlier. Unfortunately, I had to return to Salisbury District Hospital for this appointment.

The dental examinations confirmed that there was nothing wrong with my tooth or with the related nerves. I returned to the doctor, still complaining of the persistent headache. I didn't want to admit what I thought was the cause, and just started crying. I didn't want her think that I was going crazy. She pulled her chair up to me and said, "What do you want to say? Do you think that you have a brain tumour?"

"Yes, Ma'am," I replied.

She held my hands and looked straight into my eyes and said, "Just for you, to settle your mind and to let you feel comfortable, I am going to book an appointment for you to have a brain scan done."

"I don't want to go back to Salisbury District Hospital", I told her.

"No, I won't send you back to Salisbury District Hospital. I am making the appointment at the Royal United Hospital in Bath."

Michael had written a detailed letter of complaint about the treatment I had received, which had resulted in the miscarriage of our baby while on the hospital ward, and the subsequent treatment that I received post-miscarriage. We received a reply from the then chief executive, stating in essence that they would review their procedures so that a similar situation does not recur. Michael had also sent copies of the complaint to the senior medical officer and to the commanding officer for the regiment.

Following the reply from the chief executive at the Salisbury District Hospital, my personal care at the medical centre was taken over by the senior medical officer, Colonel Mike Hood. Not that the care I received from them previously was inadequate, but I believe that he intervened after also receiving a copy of the response from the chief executive at Salisbury District Hospital.

Colonel Hood rang and invited Michael and me for a consultation. He asked how I was feeling; if I had been eating and sleeping well, and I told him, "No, not really." He proposed sending me for an assessment at the Department of Community Mental Health (DCMH) at the Army facility in Tidworth, Wiltshire.

Michael accompanied me to the mental health assessment in Tidworth, but he was told that he could not actually sit in the meeting with me. It was the first opportunity that I had properly had to talk about what really happened. I saw a male mental health nurse, who did a fantastic job listening to all I had to say. I went through all the events, from being admitted to the hospital from July 29; the miscarriage; and being in and out of hospital for two weeks subsequently. I cried and cried. I missed my baby so much. Why? Why did I have to lose her?

14

After the miscarriage, one of my greatest challenges was going out in public because of the perceived shame of losing the baby. On one occasion, Michael and I were in a shop in Bristol, where we normally bought our Jamaican food. One of the ladies who worked there came over to us and asked, "Where is the baby?" in a friendly tone of voice. Michael and I then looked at each other, as if we were in a daze, and I walked hurriedly away, sobbing. This was the kind of thing I'd feared happening: being asked time and again by different people about the baby. Michael bravely told her that we had lost the baby. This was a difficult day for me, but my husband did his best to deal with this situation and to comfort me.

Since I suffered the miscarriage, one of the strangest things that I had noticed was the number of pregnant women I would see in the shopping centres or on the streets. I had never noticed so many pregnant women before. I remember going into a store in the shopping centre in Bristol, and it seemed like every other woman who came through the doors was pregnant. This was difficult to deal with, to be honest. It seemed like everyone else was having a happy pregnancy while my baby had gone. I did my best to avoid baby sections in stores as much as I possibly could.

Although I had gone through a horrible sequence of events, the reality was that I now had to consider returning to work. The compassionate posting away from the regiment in Warminster, which the RAO had suggested, was being finalised. He had mentioned that it would be good for me to get a posting at a regiment within thirty or so miles from Bristol, where Michael worked.

I knew that there was a regiment in Colerne, near Chippenham, which was just off the M4 motorway and approximately within thirty miles of Bristol. I made a few telephone calls to find out if there was any opportunity for me to work there. I rang the regimental headquarters and, to my surprise, the person who answered had a distinct Jamaican accent. I was taken aback at first, but proceeded to make some enquiries about the regiment. She confirmed that she was indeed Jamaican and was, like me, a military clerk. She informed me that there was a vacancy for a junior clerk, and suggested that I ask my boss to submit a posting order, requesting transfer to the 21 Signal Regiment.

I thought long and hard about returning to work, and came to the conclusion that work would allow me to get back to some degree of normalcy. This compassionate posting was intended to shift my focus away from what I had been through, and onto a gradual return to normal.

The posting came through, and I was transferred to 21 Signal Regiment approximately two weeks before I resumed work. I was quite delighted at this, as it was a relatively easy commute for Michael to get to work near the Royal Portbury Dock, just off the M5 motorway.

The removal guys came and did the packing, and took our belongings to be delivered to the new Army married quarters the next day. We stayed overnight at a bed and breakfast.

This Army quarter was a three-bedroom house, which was more spacious than the one we previously had in Warminster. It took us a while to unpack all our belongings, but we were getting used to the fact I was in the Army, and that we would be required to move around a lot, so it might sometimes take a little while for us to be fully settled.

The married quarters were adjacent to the camp, so it was an easy five-minute walk to the regimental headquarters (RHQ). A couple of days before returning to work, I went over to meet the RAO and Det commander. The RAO was not present, so I only saw the Det commander. Instead of taking me to his office, he spoke to me in a corridor. "How are you feeling now?" he asked.

"Still feeling a bit ill," I replied.

"You are going to get better soon, yeah?"

Fighting back the tears, I replied "Yes, sir." I started thinking to myself, 'What is this man like? This is supposed to be compassionate posting!' Perhaps I was expecting too much; this was a male-dominated environment, and perhaps I wasn't expected to be 'emotional' or 'maternal' after losing my child under the circumstances that I had.

I was aware that I was a soldier, but I just lost my baby. To me, I had lost a loved one, and had the right to grieve for my child. I just wanted the opportunity to gradually get back into the flow of things. I thought that, having been given a compassionate posting, this would have been the case.

I returned to work on October 18, 2005, and was determined to be positive, to immerse myself into my work, and to put the loss of the baby behind me as much as possible.

I met the RAO, who informed me that the regiment was currently being inspected. He told me that I was going to be working in RHQ to help with the inspection, so I would be working with the document clerk.

Approximately two weeks into the posting, they started moving me around a lot. Some days, I worked in the post room and other times I was in a squadron, so there was no stability. While this was happening, it seemed as if my mental health was deteriorating. I found that I wasn't able to concentrate on my job, and started to be quite tearful and agitated most of the time.

Even though I described to the doctors all the different symptoms I was experiencing, there wasn't the same level of care that I had experienced from the doctors at the LWTC (Land Warfare Training Centre) in Warminster. I am not sure that my medical files had been forwarded to the Signal Regiment's medical centre from Warminster, however. Being a clerk, I knew that medical documentation moved through the system quite slowly.

My condition appeared to be getting worse by the day. I wasn't eating much, and I had no desire for food, as it seemed like everything was bland. I also found it difficult to sleep at nights, because my mind was just reliving all that I been through over and over again. It seemed that members of the Det started to watch my every move while I was at work. This was intensely pressuring. I am sure that I was not being paranoid about this. I remember one day, they sent me to work in the post room with one of the civilian workers. We had dealt with all the morning post, and there wasn't much to do after that, so I started flicking through an old magazine when two senior clerks rushed in. One of the girls started shouting, "What are you doing? Is this what we sent you down here to do, to read magazines?"

I calmly replied, "I am not reading; I am just flicking through."

"You are lying!" she shouted again. "I'm going to tell the chief clerk what you are getting up to," she continued, and stormed off.

Five minutes later, the phone rang and it was the chief clerk. He said that he wanted to talk to me. When I went to his office, both senior clerks were there, along with the chief clerk. He didn't seem interested, but the corporal was laying into me and continued to call me a liar. I calmly said to her that I wasn't a liar. And the chief just told me not to do it again. I didn't see what the problem was; everybody in the office flicked through magazines from time to time. They also took lots of cigarette breaks, which I didn't do because I didn't smoke. This was the level of unwarranted scrutiny I was having to endure, while many others were having an easy time. Why was this? I didn't know.

The preparation for the inspection was still continuing, and I found myself doing as much as everyone else, working into the night and at the weekends. I started asking myself whether this was a compassionate posting. To be fair, I didn't mind this at first, because I thought that working intensely for long hours would take my mind off losing the baby but, sadly, this was not the case. It became overly pressuring and I continued to get progressively worse. I found that my mind would just run and run, and I was not able to shut it down. I became very frantic and scared about this, as I started developing some very dark thoughts. I didn't know what was happening at the time; I thought that I was just grieving, as that was what the counsellor at the Department of Community Mental Health (DCMH) had told me. He informed me that it would have been normal for me to feel the way I did, but thinking back now, I had been getting progressively worse from the

SURVIVAL AGAINST THE ODDS

time of the appointment at the DCMH. It seemed that pressure at work had only made matters worse. I honestly did not know what was happening to me! All I could think was that I was becoming mad.

One afternoon, I was at home alone, and I suddenly started to feel extremely hot. I was perspiring down my back and chest; my feet felt cold; my hands were sweating. My head felt as if it was spinning, and I heard a voice telling me to take all my clothes off and just run outside. What held me back from doing this was another voice, one telling me to draw strength from my Christian faith. This was an even stronger, conflicting voice, saying, "Don't do this, Necola." Deep inside my subconscious, while this struggle was continuing, I could hear certain Scriptures replaying in my mind. Scriptures such as: "And we know that all things work together for good to them that love God, to them who are the called according to His purpose" (Romans 8:28 KJV), and "I will never leave thee, nor forsake thee" (Hebrews 13:5 KJV).

When the Scriptures started replaying in my mind, it was if the darkness pervading over me was lifted, and I regained consciousness. I started to feel a deep sense of shame and embarrassment of the thoughts that had been running through my head. I kept repeating to myself that a born again Christian should not allow themselves to go to that level of mental breakdown.

I sat on the top of the stairs, with my face in my hands, asking the Lord for forgiveness, and for Him to hold me, or I might lose my mind. While this had been happening, Michael was away at work in Bristol. I wished he could have been home to comfort me.

It must have been difficult for Michael as well. He, too, had lost his child, and was there with me throughout this entire ordeal. He remained remarkably strong the whole time, and the support that he gave to me was mainly outstanding. It felt reassuring to have his shoulders to cry on, as he encouraged me time and again.

He is a strong believer, and a man of great faith in Jesus Christ. I can remember one day he said to me that I shouldn't allow what has happened to cause me to lose my mind because, someday, in the not too distant future, God was going to bless me with a wonderful family, and I was going to need a strong mind to take care of them. I sincerely wanted to believe this, but at that time, this seemed so far-fetched.

It was as if my mind didn't want me to believe this. Instead, since the hospital kept telling me that the miscarriage was a direct result of the fibroid, I often had the fear that even if I became pregnant again, the same thing would happen all over again.

15

At work, the pressure intensified. I just could not believe some of the things that were happening to me. I was struggling to cope with the workload and especially with the extra level of scrutiny.

I described my symptoms to the doctors at the medical centre, but nothing meaningful was done. I didn't get the impression that there was a care plan in place for me; everything just seemed ad hoc. The unfortunate thing for me also was that I was not permitted to go and see a civilian doctor off camp, as whatever they decided would have been overridden by the medical centre.

My work output was bad. I can remember that one Friday I was the duty clerk for the weekend, which meant that I should have waited until the Royal Mail postman came to take the day's mail from the regiment, but I was feeling really ill, and everyone had left for the day. I waited for what seemed to me a long time to see if anyone would return for anything, but no one did. I totally forgot about the mail and just went home.

Monday, I went into the office very early and opened up the building, and waited until the next duty clerk arrived. I handed over the keys and the phone, and left for my squadron.

At approximately 9.30 am, I received a call from the SSA, the person responsible for discipline in the regiment. Honestly, I was quite nervous about what he could be calling me about. I had never had disciplinary issues, so I concluded that it must have been something I had or had not done over the weekend.

When I got to his office, he told me that Friday's mail was still in the building, as I hadn't been present to hand the post over to the postman. He outlined how serious this type of error was, and proceeded to inform me that there would be consequences for such an error of judgment. He told me that they were giving me three additional days as duty clerk as punishment.

I was devastated. How could I have made such a stupid error? I indeed appreciated the magnitude of the error, and its potential implications on another person's life, however.

By the time I was notified of the error, almost all the other clerks had already been made aware. I kept away from everybody else, and was pretty hard on myself.

This left me feeling low and disillusioned about all I was going through – all over again. It was very intense, as if my mind had started to play games on me, pushing me further into a dark place that I had not wanted to experience ever again. I felt alone and isolated, which contributed to me feeling anxious.

I soon realised that I couldn't bear to hear any sort of loud noise – including the telephone and doorbell. I realised, on the Bonfire Night that year that I was getting ill. Michael and I were at home when all the fireworks and banging sounds were going off all around. The regiment didn't have an official bonfire event as such, but I believe one had been organised in the village approximately one kilometre away from where we lived. The majority of the banging sounds were coming from that direction, and still I was in a panic.

My life became even more difficult at work, as I was informed by the Detachment commander that they were planning to send me back to training school, so I could redo my initial clerk course. This was devastating and humiliating, to say the least. I knew that I was a hardworking and effective clerk, and was determined that I wasn't going back to Worthy Down to redo this course – keeping in mind that I had been told that this was supposedly a compassionate posting. I was suffering as a result of losing my unborn child – combined with the ridiculously horrifying care – and their solution was to send me back on a course.

When Michael arrived home, I told him what they had said. I was very tearful, as I was wondering why they had wanted to humiliate me in this way. Michael told me not to worry, as he would put the whole situation to the Lord in prayer. A week later, Michael's prayer was answered, as I was told by the Det commander that I could do a refresher at work, instead of going back to training school. This was a much better solution as far as I was concerned, but I was still saddened at having to do the course again.

Losing my baby, the lack of appropriate care at the Salisbury District Hospital, and now this pressure, it seemed all too much for me. I started having regular panic attacks; if we went out, I would refuse to enter the house again. I would just sit in the car for a long time, fighting the fear that I had. I dreaded going into my bedroom especially. My mind was telling me that something was there to hurt me. The closet was opposite the bed and, whenever I looked into it, it seemed like some gremlin-type figures were coming out of a dark hole at me.

I can remember one day Michael said something to me that I wasn't expecting. He looked straight into my eyes, and said in a stern voice, "I don't like how you are looking; your eyes are looking very wild, and your face looks pale. I don't want any zombie in here!" I was shocked at this outburst from him. I hated him at that moment. I cried. 'How could he have spoken to me like that?' I thought to myself. I was sure that he was concerned about me, but I couldn't see things from his perspective. All I knew was that I missed my baby, that I was getting mad and didn't know what to do. My mum was in the house at the time, and she too started expressing concern that I was allowing the loss of the baby to cause me to go crazy.

I don't know why I didn't get any help from the medical centre. I told the doctors all I had been experiencing, but they didn't treat me with anti-depressants. As a result of this, I decided to deal with the matter on my own, which I believe caused my mental health to deteriorate.

I remember I started thinking about the pills the doctor offered me in Warminster, and how I could get hold of them to take now. I thought I couldn't go to the doctors at 21 Signal Regiment and ask for anti-depressants, what would they think of me diagnosing myself with depression? I did not know how to go about asking the doctor about getting them. I started thinking that, if I began taking these tablets, I would be letting the Lord down for not depending on Him for my healing. I also started thinking that I was a weak Christian. There was a thought that I was demon-possessed, with all the voices in my head and the things that they were telling me to do.

I began thinking back to how I was before all this started happening to me, and I realised that my mind was normal; I could regulate my thought processes and shut down my mind at will. Losing the baby was a terrible shock to the system and, over the subsequent weeks, I had gradually lost control over my mind. I believe this was caused from the trauma of losing the baby, and the dismissive way I was dealt with by the consultant and others at Salisbury District Hospital, when pieces of placenta were left inside of me.

From time to time, different people from our church would call in support. One day, I was at home and I received a call from an older church sister. She said, "Don't let the doctor give you any of those tablets, those depression ones." She continued, "Because you are not going 'wacko', and once you go on them, you have to depend on them for life."

I was shocked to hear this. "No, no, no," I said hastily. I started to think that this was a confirmation from the Lord that I should depend on Him for my healing. This also demonstrated the stigma in the community towards mental health.

Mummy, Teisha, Sadie and me (in the foreground) along with Uncle Fred and cousins at Norman Manley Airport in Jamaica

Me, just prior to going on a run when preparing to join the Army

Teisha and me after my Passing Out parade

Packing to go to Iraq

On a Chinook helicopter in Iraq

Me and my dear Grandma, Cecelia, at her home in St Thomas, Jamaica

16

I started regretting being transferred from Warminster, as I thought that, had I still been there, I would have received a much higher standard of care.

I became very fearful of knives. I usually loved being in the kitchen, and suddenly I didn't trust being by myself with knives around, as I feared that I would hurt myself or someone else.

Thinking back now, I am ashamed to mention that I also had no interest in keeping the house tidy. At times, the kitchen sink and worktop were filled with dirty pots and pans. On two different occasions, we had help from two different Jamaican girls, who we had become close to. Sometimes I didn't let them in, due to the state of the place, but they were persistent, and came and washed the dishes and tidied the rest of the downstairs area. I will forever be thankful to Felecia and Barbara for their labour of love.

At that point, all I wanted to do was to get to Jamaica, though. It was late November and it was now cold and grey most of the time. I felt that this weather had also started to get me really down. I can't remember the grey and coldness having such an impact on my mood before.

I felt a deep sense of hopelessness, but knew that if I went to Jamaica, then the church brethren there would pray for me, and I would receive my deliverance. I planned to work over the Christmas season and take a vacation with Michael in early January 2006, returning on the same flight along with my mother.

One of the major hurdles I had to face was to get past Hope's official due date, which was December 30. The usual excitement that would be in our house at that time of the year sadly did not exist. Before the loss of Hope, Christmas had been a big thing for me. I would normally go the full shebang in the usual Jamaican way: Christmas tree, lights, decorations, cakes, ham, sorrel juice, changing the curtains and bedspreads.

A couple of days before the due date came, I was replaying in my mind the joy that we had felt, when we found out that I was pregnant. It was a special feeling; I had felt privileged and blessed. We were in a happy place and were ready for parenthood. But now, I felt as if I had been robbed of my opportunity to be a loving and caring mother. I thought about how different things should have been. Now, however, my childhood dream of having my own family had been dashed, and I was in a position where I wasn't even sure I could be pregnant again.

The time came for us to go to Jamaica. Previously, whenever I was about to go to Jamaica, I would be so excited. I would start the countdown months before, and whenever the actual time came, I would be head over heels with excitement. This time, it was different, though. I just wanted to go to get my healing, and to draw strength from the rest of my family out there.

I arrived in Jamaica and the mood was very low. The flight lasted nine hours, and I don't believe that I even had thirty minutes sleep during that time. My mind just kept running, once again repeating all the events that had led up to the miscarriage, and the subsequent events at the hospital and at work.

We spent about two days at my parents' home before going to Couples Hotel, where we stayed for three nights, but this didn't change my mood at all.

Michael tried his best to encourage me to let myself go and enjoy the ambiance, as I normally would; all his efforts were unsuccessful, though. In fact, I could not wait to get away from the place. The environment was not helping, as all the previous times I had been there had been under much happier circumstances. To me, that place symbolised happiness and fun, but now I was just missing my baby, and was a mental wreck.

We left the hotel, and returned to my parents' home. All I was thinking about was getting prayed for, in order to receive my deliverance, which would have made me better.

The Holy Spirit showed me the person that I should go to for prayer, which was Michael's godmother. She was a powerful woman of God, and I had full confidence that she could help. I didn't share this with Michael initially, though, as I knew that he didn't want his godmother to know that I was mentally ill. I kept telling Michael that I needed to go and talk to her, but he was very reluctant for me to do so.

After badgering him for some time, he relented and we both went to see 'Goddie'. We went to her house and she was very excited to see us. After the formalities of meeting up, we sat on the verandah, and began sharing what had happened to me. The atmosphere was just so clear and she allowed me to express myself so freely, that as I spoke the tears were just flowing. After sharing the experiences with her for about an hour, she ushered me into her living room, and started to pray for me. When she started to pray, I started throwing up; I started to see things differently. It was as though the scales were being removed from my eyes. The sun seemed brighter; Michael looked even more handsome; things just seemed different, as if a load had lifted off me. I immediately started to say, "Thank You, Jesus. Thank You, Jesus," repeating this over and over, and getting stronger all the time. I've never experienced this before, and couldn't have known what would happen when I left the UK for Jamaica. All I knew was that I needed prayer. Initially, I believed that I would actually be prayed for in church, but the Lord directed me to Michael's godmother, and she was instrumental in my deliverance.

I am extremely grateful to Minister Mercle Jones-Moodie – 'Goddie' – for allowing herself to be used by the Lord in this way, in helping me to receive my healing.

After this, I started to view what had happened to us in a more spiritual than emotional light, which enabled me to be more positive, and I started to become more grateful to the Lord that I was alive and, as a result, had the opportunity to have more children. This experience had taught me that Jesus Christ had been with me through the many ordeals, and that the Word of God had become my comfort and solace. 'Goddie' had reminded me to read the Book of Psalms for encouragement, which I started to do in earnest.

This was extremely beneficial to me, as each time the negative thoughts and emotions came over me, I would reject these thoughts by quoting the Scriptures from Psalms, a few of the favourite ones were: "Weeping may endure for a night, but joy cometh in the morning" (Psalm 30:5). Another was "Be of good courage, and He shall strengthen your heart, all ye that hope in the Lord" (Psalm 31:24) and "Why art thou cast down, O my soul? And why art thou disquieted in me? Hope thou in God: for I shall yet praise Him for the help of His countenance" (Psalm 42:5).

The Psalms were a great source of strength and were inspirational for me on my road to recovery.

However, there were moments when I still felt quite low, and just didn't want to do normal activities. I instead wanted to lie in bed and at times felt like I wanted to die. There were good and bad days, but at the time it seemed that the bad days far outweighed the good ones.

While we were in Jamaica, we learned that my paternal grandmother, Mrs Cecelia Watson (or 'Miss Sissie', as she was affectionately known), was also in the country on holiday from the United States, along with my Aunty Evelyn. Grandma had emigrated from Jamaica to the US some years before. She had lived in St Thomas, about five kilometres from the capital of that parish, Morant Bay.

Even though my father had had a fractured relationship with his own mother, this hadn't affected my relationship with her. She was a source of stability and dependability in my life as a child. She had treated me with the utmost care, attention and love, which had made me feel special. So, no matter what my father had said about her, this had not affected my impression of her, as she had shown me a totally different side of his perception of her.

Before emigrating to the United States, she worked as a live-in household helper with a family in the Barbican area of St Andrew. At this stage, she must have been in her late fifties. She rented a house just down the road from where we lived. My weekend started when she arrived back home. She would take home a lot of treats for me, such as bread puddings and an assortment of food that she brought home from work. She was a very excellent cook; her pepper pot soup was the best. She is now 89 years old, still travels to Jamaica every winter, and still cooks up a storm.

I remembered that she was a prayer warrior. Whenever she began to pray no one could sleep in the house, as she would pray very loudly for hours upon hours. She and I attended many national conventions of the Church of God of Prophecy at the National Arena together. This woman dedicated her life to the Lord, and she had inspired me to do the same, in having a deep relationship with God. When she emigrated to the United States, I was so devastated, as my loving grandma – who had spoilt me – had gone!

The special relationship we had bore much fruit as, when I was getting married in 1999, Aunty Evelyn and Grandma supported me extensively. They provided my beautiful dress and supplied the exquisite invitations, as well as other cash gifts, and gave me the ultimate honour of attending my wedding.

Just speaking about my wedding day brought back great excitement and joy. Everything had gone very well, apart from the fact that Michael was an hour late and I had to be driven around all that time. I eventually forgave him, although I still remind him of this at every opportunity.

I received tremendous support from all the members of my immediate family. In addition to my grandma and Aunty Evelyn, several of my mothers' siblings had come from Canada and the USA to support us. Aunty Muriel again played the grandmother role on my maternal side, and she was duly aided by my uncles, Johnny and Earl.

My father was not to be outdone, and he pulled out all the stops to make my wedding a success. He made it possible for our reception to be held on the grounds of the picturesque Jamaica Maritime Training Institute (now the Caribbean Maritime Institute), located on the Palisados Road, near the Norman Manley Airport in Kingston.

Daddy had worked tirelessly in the kitchen all day, and provided all the food and refreshments, including baking my wedding cake. He was also on time to walk me down the aisle, and handed me over to Michael. "Who gives away this bride?" the minister asked. "I do," he answered loudly and proudly, to an outburst of laughter from the congregation. My dad came through for me on my wedding day, and his little girl was very happy. I knew he had it in him.

We arrived at the house about 11.30 am, and were greeted by Grandma and Aunty Evelyn and her young children, who were running with abandon, round and round the yard with one of the many resident puppies. We chatted about being in the Army, going to Iraq and the loss of the pregnancy, amongst other things. Later in the afternoon, we had lunch, especially prepared by my eighty-year-old grandmother; it was simply great! Ackee and salt fish, boiled dumplings and yams.

After such a wholesome lunch, all I wanted to do was to find somewhere comfortable to have a nap. Aunty Evelyn called Michael and me away from Grandma and the others, into her bedroom. When I found a comfortable spot to sit on the bed, she asked, "How are you feeling?" "Yeah, fine, I guess," I muttered. Michael then left the room, allowing us to continue our aunty-to-niece conversation in private.

When Michael was out of earshot, she asked again, "How are you really feeling?"

"To be honest, Aunty, I am not doing very well at all" I replied, with tears flowing down the sides of my face. She then said to me that she knew that I hadn't been well; all of her pregnancies had been successful, and yet she had still suffered postnatal depression. She said that I didn't get to take home my baby, so I must have been affected by my loss. This was the first time I had heard the term 'postnatal depression'.

Aunty Evelyn then called for Michael to rejoin us in the bedroom. She said to him, "Michael, don't you see that Necola is sick?"

"She will be fine," he replied, unsurely. I then said to her that I'd already been prayed for by Michael's godmother.

She responded, "Yes, prayer is good, but you need medical intervention. For what you have been through, you really do need the medical help along with the prayer."

She then said that I should not feel embarrassed to go to the doctor to get help. "No, Aunty," I replied quietly. She wanted to know if I would go and see a doctor in Morant Bay. We both looked at each other, then Michael told her that we would go.

She called her brother, who is also one of my uncles, for him to come and take us into town. He came within twenty minutes of the call. When we arrived at the doctor's surgery, there were about three patients waiting to be seen before us. Happily it wasn't long before it was my turn.

All three of us went in to see the doctor. My aunt introduced Michael, and I went on to explain the situation to him. He asked me a few questions about what had happened to me and how I was feeling. He prescribed anti-depressant tablets for me, and told me that I should go and see my doctor as soon as I returned to the UK. He gave me a sealed letter to give to them. He advised me that the tablets would take up to two weeks to start working.

The Lord is so faithful to me, in that I went to Jamaica with the intention of getting prayer and support from the church brethren, and ended up being prayed for by Michael's godmother and getting that spiritual deliverance. Furthermore, I had no idea that a visit to my grandmother would have led to me being taken by my aunt to see a doctor and being prescribed anti-depressants. I was extremely happy for the Lord's providence, and for the love and support from my Aunty Evelyn. I felt a sense of hope that I could now start rebuilding my life by putting the miscarriage behind me, and cope better with my mental health issues.

17

I returned to the UK at the end of January, and went to work a few days later. My priority at this stage of my life, though, was to get the appropriate help for my mental health.

I followed the advice of the doctor in Jamaica, and made an appointment to see the GP at the medical centre at 21 Signal Regiment. I gave the GP the letter from the doctor in Jamaica, and explained what had been happening to cause me to visit the doctor in Jamaica.

I told him that when I was in Warminster I was sent to the DCMH in Tidworth. I spoke about the miscarriage, and they concluded that I was just grieving the loss of my baby. The doctor took a look at my file, and said to me that, according to the report, it was more than grieving that I had been experiencing. I was so surprised to have heard this and asked, "Why wasn't I told this before? Why did no one try to help me before now?" I then thought to myself that if my aunt had not told me of her own experiences, and had not taken me to the doctor in Jamaica, I would not have known that what I was currently experiencing was postnatal depression. He responded that he wasn't aware that I hadn't been treated for that.

I could understand the doctor's surprise; there were three different civilian doctors, who worked at the medical centre on camp on different days, unlike Warminster Primary Care Centre. There wasn't, for example, a permanent doctor who was familiar with me and with my condition to offer the appropriate level of care. In addition, I was new to the regiment, having been posted there only three months earlier, in October.

He put me on a course of anti-depressants and made another appointment for me to return to see him. I was very happy that I was now receiving the care I had been desperate for.

In addition to this, a friend of ours lent me a book, which totally transformed my thinking and coping mechanisms. The title of this book is *The Battlefield of the Mind* by Joyce Meyer. This book gave me some practical ways on how to cope with the many things that were going through my mind. My coping mechanism was to start rejecting the loss of my baby in my mind by using Scriptures such as, "The Lord gave and the Lord hath taken away; blessed be the Name of the Lord." (Job 1:21 KJV)

I was lying in bed one Sunday morning at about 9.00 am, as I wasn't feeling well, when I heard Michael shouting for me, and frantically running up the stairs. "Necola, look!" he shouted. "Look at this Scripture!" I had absolutely no idea what he was referring to, as he had gone to the living room to have his devotion, as he hadn't wanted to disturb me.

He came bursting into the bedroom, panting, with his Bible in hand, "Listen to this," and he read:

> The children born during your bereavement will yet say in your hearing, "This place is too small for us; give us more space to live in." Then you will say in your heart, "Who bore me these? I was bereaved and barren; I was exiled and rejected. Who brought these up? I was left all alone, but these – where have they come from?" (Isaiah 49:20-21 NIV)

Michael was beside himself with excitement, "Darling, do you know what this means?" he asked rhetorically. "The Lord is saying that we are going to have children, because we are in our bereavement and to get this Scripture today," after a brief pause he continued, "I am sure that I have read this Scripture many times before, and it is the first time I am seeing this."

We received this prophetic word by faith, and started to worship the Lord in anticipation of what He was about to do for us. This was not an easy time for us, and to receive such a definitive word was hugely reassuring and comforting. We just worshipped the Lord and thanked Him for this divine revelation.

After I had had the miscarriage, the GP at the barracks in Warminster had referred me to a consultant gynaecologist at the St Michael's Hospital in Bristol. Salisbury District Hospital had stated in their report that it was the large fibroid that had been the direct cause of the miscarriage. The referral was made for the team in Bristol to explore ways in preventing anything like this happening again in the future.

We went in for a consultation, and saw the consultant gynaecologist, who was quite caring and considerate. He made it clear that, since it had been said that it was the fibroid that had caused the miscarriage, then the best solution was to have it removed. He also stressed the massive risks that such a major surgery involved, and mentioned that, because the fibroid was classified as a degenerating one, there was the possibility that there might be excessive bleeding during or after the surgery, which might result in a myomectomy. This type of surgery meant that they would have to remove my uterus, making it impossible for me to give birth to children of my own.

This was devastating news and very difficult to take on board. I felt physically sick on hearing this information. That was not the end of my potential worries, however. He further added that, after the surgery, there was a potential risk that the walls of the uterus might become weak, due to whatever incision was made into it during surgery. Therefore, as any future pregnancy progressed, this could result in multiple miscarriages, again significantly affecting my ability to have children. This was too much for me; it felt like I was being tortured.

After he had given us this information, he gave us the opportunity to ask questions regarding the myomectomy. I asked a few questions in relation to the possibility of losing my ability to have my own child if things were to go wrong during surgery. He was quite reassuring that the potential for things to go wrong didn't mean that it would actually happen, but he had to tell us the risks involved.

He further added that, since the fibroid was currently the size of a small grapefruit about ten centimetres in diameter, he would give me hormone treatment in the form of injections that would be given every twenty-eight days. This would be a three-course treatment (I believe it was GnRH) to cause the fibroid to shrink before the surgery, in order to reduce the risks. The ultimate decision on whether the surgery went ahead lay with me. I now had to weigh up all the risks and take the decision along with Michael. We had long and deep discussions about all the possibilities, and this felt like a great burden on my shoulders. I was in utter turmoil and anguish at the thought that I could lose my uterus if something went wrong during surgery.

Michael did extensive research on the Internet in an effort to satisfy himself that we had understood the gravity of what we were potentially going to undertake. At first, I was very fearful about the whole thing, and found it difficult to eat or sleep. This decision was consuming my whole life.

During this whole episode, Michael and I were faithful to attend church, though, feeding on the Word of God. We didn't miss prayer meetings or Bible studies, and increased our faith in God and in His ability to help us. I remember that one of Michael's former managers, at the building society where he worked in Jamaica, had said to us that we should pray again. We had already prayed for the baby that we had lost, and we should pray again for the Lord to restore us. This was a simple but powerful statement, I believe. I held on to these words, and prayed for the Lord's restoration of my child.

There were times when we couldn't do the long prayers, so Michael suggested that we did what we called 'chain prayers'. We would kneel on opposite sides of the bed, holding each other's hands, and prayed alternately for a maximum of thirty to forty seconds each. We did this for up to fifteen or twenty minutes every day.

We did little things to improve our faith, as this decision about the surgery was a big one, and could be absolutely life-changing. The mother of one of our church sisters came over from Jamaica. This sister was a member of the cell group that Michael led. Her mother learnt of my miscarriage and of the large fibroid that I was carrying.

One day, we had a chat in church and she said to me, "Don't make the fibroid bigger than God." Again, this came across to me quite powerfully; I accepted what she said, and started to pray accordingly.

By about April 2006, I started to feel much better mentally, as I believe the anti-depressants had started to work. My performance at work gradually improved, which also had a positive impact on my self-esteem and on my interaction with others. When I was ill, I wasn't interested in socialising with people in the slightest, but now I was a much happier woman.

Michael continued to fast and pray about the big decision that we had to take regarding surgery, and asked the Lord for divine intervention in the form of healing. I wasn't able to fast, so I supported him in prayer.

One Saturday evening, we were at home when Michael said to me, "The Lord has told me to do something, but you might think that I am crazy." I thought to myself, 'What was he coming with now?' He took his Bible and read the Scriptures from 2 Kings 4.

He anointed me all over with olive oil, especially the area where the fibroid was, and then told me to lie on my back with my arms stretched wide and, just as Elisha did in the Scriptures, he lay upon me, covering all parts of my body with his. He got up and prayed, and did the same three times. After that, we got up and embraced each other, and asked the Lord to honour His Word and our faith.

About a week later, I was lying in bed and the Holy Spirit said to me, "This time next year you are going to have a son. Put this everywhere you go in the house, and read it out every time you see it." I was sure it was the Holy Spirit and, as a result, I immediately jumped off the bed and took my Bible to find the Scripture in Genesis 18:10, where the Lord spoke to Abraham. I went to the computer and typed it out repeatedly. I placed it on the wall next to my bed; the inside of the bathroom door; on the fridge; on the television, and many other places around the house where I knew I would see it. This was a reminder of God's promise to me, and I held onto this as if my life depended on it.

I desperately wanted to have a child for my husband. So, I started praying the Scriptures, reminding the Lord of His promises through the Word that he gave Michael, and the Word, which He gave to me.

After wrestling with the decision, I decided by God's help to go ahead with the surgery. Taking such a decision was not easy, but I trusted in the Lord. I remembered what the sister from Jamaica had said to me, that I should not make the fibroid bigger than my God. I told myself that my God is Lord; He is Lord over my body and over the fibroid, and if He wanted me to be pregnant and have a child with the fibroid still inside me, then it would happen, and if He wanted the fibroid out, the surgery would be successful, and I will be pregnant and have a child with the fibroid out. That was my resolve.

18

It was an anxious time for us, as we approached the appointment for me to have the first course of hormonal treatment. I became very desperate to be pregnant again before the treatment started. Each month my period came, I was bitterly disappointed and hurt, but took comfort from my faith in God that He is God, and would allow me to have a child with or without this fibroid.

We drove down to Bristol with the confidence that God was with us. I became sad, though, when I arrived at St Michael's Hospital, and we had to go to the department that dealt with myomectomies and hysterectomies. This was very significant to me as, just along the next corridor, was the lift that took you to Obstetrics, where the antenatal clinics were taking place. I was angry that I had the horrible fibroid inside me, without it I would not have been in this situation.

On the one hand, when I looked on the faces of the other patients in the Gynaecology department, like mine their demeanour was generally sad; these were mainly older women.

In contrast, however, when I looked on the faces of most of couples going to the antenatal clinics, their faces reflected a picture of hope and excitement, even if some expectant mothers were showing signs of discomfort. This was an extremely difficult experience for me, even though deep down I believed that somehow God would come through for me.

After sitting nervously for about half an hour in the waiting room, we were called in by the senior nurse. She did a few checks, including a pregnancy test to ensure that I wasn't pregnant, as the hormonal treatment could be damaging to the baby. She advised me that I would not have a period over the next three months, and that I would be starting to feel menopausal, which meant that I would experience hot flushes and become easily irritable at times. She then went ahead and gave me the injection, and later set the date for the next appointment. She gave me a telephone number to call if I experienced any adverse effects to the treatment.

We returned home and I carried on with my life as normal. I couldn't wait for the next appointment to come for another course of treatment. I just wanted the surgery to happen, so I could start having a family.

Approximately two weeks into the first course of hormonal treatment, I started feeling really lethargic and sleepy all the time. I kept telling Michael that the treatment seemed to have started to work, as I had been having these weird feelings. One day at work, I felt very sleepy to the point that I couldn't help myself, so I spread my Combat 95 field jacket under my desk and slept there during my lunch hour. One of the civilian workers returned from having her lunch and saw me sleeping under the desk. She seemed taken aback to find me sleeping there. "Necola, are you sure you are not pregnant?" she asked. "No," I replied quickly. I went on to remind her that I was on the treatment, and it was unlikely that I would become pregnant while on it. I then thought to myself that this was perhaps a side effect of the treatment.

I noticed that these feelings were getting worse every day. I kept complaining to Michael, who suggested that I ring the hospital on the number they gave us, and tell them about the symptoms I was experiencing. I eventually did that. I spoke to one of the nurses in that department, who told me that two weeks into the treatment was too soon for me to start experiencing any side effects. In addition, she said that the side effects would usually be felt after two months of starting treatment. I began to get concerned that the nurses, who had years of experience with dealing with this sort of thing, did not seem to have a clue about my symptoms.

There was a gospel concert at my church, and I went and performed a song. I tried my best to remain calm, and carried on with my normal life. I noticed that my clothes were getting a little tight, but didn't take any notice of it whatsoever. When we arrived back at home later in the evening, Michael mentioned how radiant I looked on the platform. I appreciated the comment, and thought he was just giving one of his many daily compliments.

All day Sunday, I was extraordinarily tired and sleepy. Michael then made a comment along the lines of, "Necola, I wonder if you might be pregnant?" For me, this was a bad word at this stage, as this was not something I was expecting, especially since the consultant and nurses pointed out that this was highly improbable during the course of the treatment. Improbable, because this particular treatment prevented the production of oestrogen in the body, and oestrogen is one of the hormones required in a woman to facilitate conception.

I was very apprehensive to even consider that this might be a possibility. "No," I said to Michael, "I can't be pregnant." Michael was convinced that we should go and buy a pregnancy test; I was not convinced that this was necessary, but he went ahead nonetheless. He bought one of the more expensive ones on the market, which promised that the test would give a result even if a woman were only twenty-four hours pregnant.

He returned with the test, but I couldn't touch it; I was too afraid. I didn't want to get my hopes up, just for them to be dashed again. I simply put it down in the bathroom. Michael was more philosophical and pragmatic, however. He said to me, laughingly, in his Jamaican accent, "Well, if you are pregnant today, you will be more pregnant tomorrow, so leave it till first thing in the morning."

I got up while Michael was downstairs getting ready to leave for work. I secretly did the test before he left. To my utter surprise, seconds after dipping the stick into the urine sample, there a clear big blue plus sign appeared in the result window.

At this point, my mind seemed to be running at an astonishingly fast pace. Within a few seconds, all kinds of different emotions swept over me. "Michael! Michael! Come and look at this!" I shouted from inside the bathroom. Michael was literally going through the door, then he came rushing up the stairs to me. "What is it?" he asked, as he entered the bathroom. I gave him the test stick and he saw the result for himself. We shouted and hugged each other and cried. These were tears of joy and relief.

Michael didn't bother going to work that day, as he decided that it would be too emotional for me to be left on my own; besides, I needed his help in getting around. I rang the medical centre and got an appointment to see the doctor. Mine was deemed such a special case that I got an urgent appointment. I did an Army medical pregnancy test, which officially confirmed that I was indeed pregnant. "I am pregnant," I whispered to Michael, while we held each other's hands tightly; it almost sounded surreal. This was the last thing I was expecting at this stage. All I was now focused on was to get the fibroid reduced, so that I could have the myomectomy done, but praise God, He had another plan. The Lord our God is faithful.

The next few hours were extremely frantic; the GP at the medical centre immediately rang the gynaecologist in Bristol to discuss the situation of me becoming pregnant. It was suggested that I might have to go over to them for an emergency consultation, because it was highly unusual for a woman to become pregnant while on the hormonal pre-treatment.

In the end, they decided that it wasn't necessary for that appointment, but they would transfer me to the care of the consultant obstetrician. Based on my recent medical history and on the circumstances of the pregnancy, I was referred to the best obstetrician at St Michael's Hospital for my care. How faithful is my God? Just two weeks previously, I had been bemoaning the fact that I had to go to the Gynaecological department of the said hospital, in preparation for surgery that could potentially be catastrophic to my ability to give birth to my own children and now, totally unexpectedly, I was going to Obstetrics like so many other expectant mothers. I was beside myself with excitement. This alone was reason to celebrate and worship my God. To me, this was a miracle. To God be the glory.

The GP told me that I should no longer take the anti-depressants, as this might be harmful to the development of the unborn child growing inside me. I thought that this could potentially cause a relapse in the progress I had made in my mental health, but I did exactly what I was advised, as I didn't want to harm my child in any way.

The doctor also warned that I was in the early stages of pregnancy, and that there was the real likelihood that I could lose the pregnancy. Despite this, I was still very confident that I would carry this pregnancy to term, based on the word that I had received from the Lord. This was my faith.

Michael and I decided to keep the pregnancy a secret until the thirteen-week mark. I only broke the news to my mother who had to be sworn to secrecy before she was told. This time we would do things differently.

About a week later, we went back to St Michael's Hospital for the appointment with the consultant obstetrician, and this time we went through the doors and headed straight for the lift to the Obstetrics department. This felt sweet; for me, this was victory.

We met the consultant obstetrician, who introduced herself. She personally did an ultrasound scan to confirm the presence of the young baby inside. I saw the little heartbeat, and my eyes welled up with tears.

She informed me that she had discussed my medical history with the consultant gynaecologist, and expressed surprise that I had got pregnant while on the hormonal treatment. She also informed me that this had been classified as a high-risk pregnancy, due to the presence of the large fibroid and the history of miscarriage. She pointed out that there was nothing they could realistically do at this stage.

The consultant also stated that there was no plan to stitch my cervix, in order to see if I would miscarry again. In fact, she said that they would allow nature to take its course before they made any medical intervention, just to see if it was the fibroid that had actually caused the first miscarriage.

I sat and listened attentively, appreciating that she was an experienced consultant, with a good reputation, and that she had to explain her observations based on her scientific knowledge. Inside I was smiling, though, because I was confident in the Word of God that I would have a son. I was definitely not making this fibroid bigger than God!

The next appointment with the consultant gynaecologist was scheduled at the fourteen-week point of the pregnancy. I guess they were making sure that the pregnancy was still viable at that stage. It was a successful appointment; the baby was growing well and everything seemed normal at this stage. The consultant informed us that in order to see if another miscarriage was likely, she would see me every fortnight to measure if there was any opening in the cervix, as the baby grew inside my womb. I was very assured by this plan, as at least I would be able to see what was happening with my cervix.

Fortnight after fortnight, Michael and I hit the M4 and M32 motorways that took us into Bristol city centre. The cost of travelling and parking charges at the hospital were mounting up, but honestly this was all very secondary. At that stage, all we wanted to know was that we were getting the requisite care that would give our baby a fighting chance to live – unlike the degradingly poor care I had received at Salisbury District Hospital.

Many times, when I turned up for my appointment, there were up to six or seven student doctors in the room, along with the consultant. On several occasions, while probing my abdomen with transducer in hand, she would fire questions at her fledgling students about the fibroid and the growth of the baby, after informing them that I had conceived while on the hormonal treatment.

For the most part, the pregnancy was developing quite well at this stage, and I was happy with the level of care I received at St Michael's Hospital. However, I was somewhat apprehensive as we approached the twenty-week point in the pregnancy, as this was the stage when we'd lost Hope. I was confident that this would not happen again, but in the back of my mind there was still a sense of fear that there was a possibility it could.

Despite having the fortnightly appointments to check whether the cervix was opening or not, I was given an appointment for the anomaly scan to check the growth and general development of the baby. For us parents, this would be the time when the medical staff could give us an idea about the sex of the child we were expecting. Thankfully, everything seemed normal with the baby, but sadly the fibroid seemed to be thriving as well.

After the more important checks were completed, this was our opportunity to potentially find out the sex of the baby. The radiographer asked if we wanted to know the sex, and we quickly replied in the affirmative. It didn't take long for it to be confirmed that we were indeed having a boy. This was the overwhelming consensus of the three of us in the room, with the male genitalia being prominently displayed by our baby.

19

The milestone of reaching the twenty-week point in the pregnancy was significant, as I had been warned repeatedly by the medical professionals that if a miscarriage was going to happen again, it would happen round about that stage.

From the time I received the word from the Lord, that I would be having a son this time next year, we agreed that our baby would be called Michael Junior – "MJ" for short. I started to relate to my baby in a more personal way, for example, referring to him by his name, and also reading to him and praying for him in the womb. This caused me to develop a bond with my baby and, to me, he became quite responsive in the womb. This was quite an exciting feeling, and the start of a special relationship between me and my unborn child.

Knowing the sex of the baby gave us the opportunity to choose clothing and the colour scheme for decorating his room.

It was still so reassuring to be having the fortnightly scans of the cervix. However, as the baby continued to grow, as with Hope, the pain from the fibroid started to increase. At times, it was more unbearable than at other times, so I now had to develop a system of coping. This meant that I had to physically endure excruciating pain for hours on end, especially whenever I was at work or just out and about.

I became reliant on co-codamol for pain relief, as this was the strongest form of pain relief the doctors were willing to give me at this stage. Personally, I was willing to endure the pain just to protect my child from being affected in any way. I felt excruciating pains at times without complaining, as I was desperate to take my precious child home this time, and would have done almost anything to make this happen.

All this time, the fibroid remained a real threat to the pregnancy, although I was having the scans of the cervix to have an idea as to what was happening. The consultant was quite happy that there were no signs of anything that she needed to be concerned about at this stage.

Just when I thought that the fibroid and the pain that derived from it were my main challenges in the pregnancy, at around the twenty-third week, I started experiencing some back pain. This gradually got worse as time progressed. One Saturday night, I was at home and couldn't move at all due to this pain. Michael decided to take me down to the hospital in Bath. I couldn't even get into the car on my own; each step forward was more unbearable than the one before. When I walked, it literally sounded like bone was clunking against bone.

Later that night, I was diagnosed with the condition known as symphysis pubis dysfunction (SPD). The doctor told me that this is a condition that sometimes happens to pregnant women, where there is an over-production of the hormone that prepares the body to give birth, wherein the ligaments become softer to allow the baby to pass more easily through the birth canal.

I was given a pair of crutches and advice about exercises to help reduce the pain, as well as tips on moving about. I was told that the pain would persist until up to eight weeks after giving birth. Now I had another physical battle on my hands to contend with, but I was determined to overcome these obstacles and to take my little prince home. I wasn't prepared to lose another child during pregnancy. I resented going back to the dark place of postnatal depression, and decided that, despite the current challenges in the pregnancy, with God's help, I would prevail this time round.

Growing up as a little girl, I had no idea that having a baby could be the challenge it was turning out to be for me. I honestly thought that it was as simple as you got pregnant and the baby is born after nine months. I am sure it was like that for a number of women, but for me it was not as straightforward.

The SPD became debilitating to the point that I became scared to go out in public. It made going out to shop for my expected baby a disenchanting and miserable affair, because of the severe pain I had to endure as soon as I left the house. Just getting into the car was a struggle. I had to sit gently then get Michael to swing my legs around. When I got to the shopping centre, for example, I would have to take very small steps, which was still very painful to do.

Going up and down the stairs was an absolute struggle for me, and being at work was really hard. The camp was large and the walk from the RHQ to the hangar where I worked was a considerable distance away. I didn't drive, and if I didn't get a lift from a friend or from one of the civilian workers and I needed a file or something, I had to walk between offices. The bones in my back would be clunking onto each other, with the pressure of the growing unborn baby pulling towards my pelvis and battling the sizeable fibroid, this felt like it was unbearable and I often cried but continued to endure.

I thought that having my family would be worth it. I didn't want to spend many years in the Army chasing a career and missing the opportunity of enjoying having a family of my own. I imagine many women of childbearing age – irrespective of their career choice – would, like me, want to rear children and have a happy family. It shouldn't be any different for me just because I was a soldier.

I received almost no support from the Detachment. In fact, I had a chit from the doctor excusing me from going on parade. On several previous occasions, I would show the chit to the manager and I would be exempt, as specified by the medical chit. On one occasion, however, there was a parade in the gym. I stayed in the office, completing my work, when my manager informed me that they were asking why I wasn't on the parade. I reminded him that I had been exempt. He said that was fine, but a few minutes later they called for me again. Then he stated that I should just go. When I arrived, the sergeant had arranged for a chair to be put down on the parade, and I had to hobble with my six-to-seven-month pregnant stomach to sit on this parade.

This man had directly overridden the authority of the doctor that I should not parade. I felt humiliated as I approached the parade, as everyone started to laugh. I went back to the doctor and told him all that had happened, and he was furious at the way I had been treated. Once again, due to my illness, it seemed as if I was public enemy number one in the regiment. Nonetheless, I struggled on as best as I could, but all these illnesses and degrading treatment were taking their toll on me physically and mentally.

While all this was happening, I also discovered that I had developed gestational diabetes. In addition to having a large, degenerating fibroid and the pain that I suffered from that, and having SPD, I now had gestational diabetes. I wondered how much more I could endure. Pre-eclampsia, perhaps? Oh, yes! I had been having a protein reading of +1 in my urine samples. At one of the antenatal appointments, it was found that my urine had a +3 protein reading and my blood pressure was quite high. The sister on duty remained calm so that we would not become too alarmed. Michael and I knew exactly what was going on, but we allowed them to execute their plan.

The sister called for an ambulance, which took me to St Michael's Hospital with blue lights. The severity of the protein reading and the elevation in blood pressure were a potentially dangerous combination, which could cause severe difficulties both for the baby and for me. I was kept in hospital and cared for by the staff, who kept the baby and me under close observation. I believe I was in hospital for about two further nights before I was allowed home. It was confirmed that I was suffering from a very dangerous condition in pregnancy, known as pre-eclampsia.

This was a real concern, but I tried my best not to worry; that was the last thing I needed, as this would just contribute to my blood pressure increasing.

Michael started researching the condition and how it affected pregnancy, and how to get through the pregnancy despite the onset of the condition. Meanwhile, I was getting larger and larger. At thirty-one to thirty-two weeks, my stomach was larger than normal, due to the large fibroid, and I looked like I was probably expecting triplets.

I had started to retain fluids, it seemed, and my feet were so swollen it was difficult for my feet to fit into normal-sized shoes. I had to wear a sturdy wide-fit leather pair whenever I went out – the only ones I felt comfortable in.

Despite the several medical challenges I had in the pregnancy up to that time, I was still extremely grateful that the baby seemed to be doing well, as all the checks had indicated. I kept holding on to my faith, believing that he would be fine and that, at last, I would have a family.

The consultant at St Michael's Hospital was getting less concerned about the cervix opening prematurely, and started to focus mainly on the pre-eclampsia and the gestational diabetes. I had earlier been put on a special diet, as they were apprehensive that the baby might become too large for a vaginal delivery, which would have meant a difficult birth. I adhered to the advice of the nutritionist, and attended all the appointments.

Even though I was suffering from all these different threatening conditions in pregnancy, including SPD, there was no sympathy shown towards me by anyone at work. In fact, the doctor had to send me to what is known as a 'half Medical Board' in Tidworth, to have me downgraded from going on parade – even at this advanced point in my pregnancy. He said that the managers could override his directive, but they could not override the directive of the Medical Board. The Medical Board took the decision to downgrade me to P0, which meant that I was deemed to be temporarily incapable of performing my duties.

I was relieved that the Medical Board had taken this view, and was also very happy that the senior medical officers had showed genuine compassion towards me when they saw the number of medical problems I had been having with this pregnancy, combined with the fact that I had quite recently suffered a miscarriage which had led to a mental breakdown. They decided that I should go on maternity leave with immediate effect, and that I should not worry about work for however long I was on maternity leave.

This meant that for the first time in my life I was on maternity leave. Sadly, with Hope, I did not get the chance to reach so far in the pregnancy; it was a dream that swiftly turned into a nightmare that will live with me forever.

I was very happy with the decision of the Medical Board. Now I was on maternity leave, there wasn't the consistent pressure that I endured from work, and I could now concentrate on taking care of the baby and myself. I was happy, too, for my dear husband, who had never flinched in his support for me in every aspect. At least he could now attend to his work without the added burden of worrying how I was coping in that grossly hostile work environment.

20

I was about thirty-five weeks pregnant, when I went on maternity leave. The consultant informed me that they would induce birth at around thirty-eight weeks of the pregnancy, in an attempt to mitigate against anything going wrong after that, due to the plethora of medical conditions now affecting me.

I became more and more immobilised due to the pains from both the fibroid and the SPD. This meant that I had to stay at home in bed most of the time. The severity of the pain when moving around meant that I couldn't even get myself down the stairs to go and watch television when Michael was not at home, because I didn't want to risk having a fall when at home by myself.

The pre-eclampsia became a real worry, as the blood pressure readings were quite high. The midwives and doctors became increasingly concerned because of the potential risk that the placenta could rupture, which would stop the flow of vital blood supply to the baby. The consultant ordered that I did a Doppler test to record the blood flow to the baby. Each time the reading seemed to be OK, but I got the impression things were getting increasingly worrying for the medical team.

One Sunday I was at home, and it was time to start getting ready for church, when I felt extremely ill. This is the worst I had felt in the pregnancy. When I told Michael he immediately said that he would not be going to church that morning. Michael was a minister in church, and hadn't taken the decision lightly not to go.

His reasoning was, however, that he didn't want to be in church, if the baby and I needed him to be at home to support us. I was there, lying on my side, breathing rather heavily, when he decided that he would ring the hospital to inform them of how I was feeling. They told him to take me in.

We arrived at the hospital at approximately 11.20 am. I was seen quite soon by a midwife, who took a urine sample and my blood pressure readings. She did a quick sounding of the baby's heartbeat, and said that it was fine, but that I needed to see a doctor.

After an hour, the doctor came and assessed me, and then he went away for about fifteen minutes. When he returned, he said, "Mrs Hall, I am sorry we will not be sending you home again until after you have given birth." I was thirty-six weeks pregnant, but the onset of the pre-eclampsia meant that the doctors were not prepared to send me home, as they wanted to monitor me closely. I wasn't overly concerned about being admitted, as my major concern was the safety and well-being of the baby.

We had been prepared for any eventuality in the pregnancy, so we were not surprised. We were advised to have a bag packed with my baby clothes and essentials, as well as my own; we kept it in the boot of the car.

I felt worse as the days in hospital went by. The doctors became more concerned about the high blood pressure readings I had been having, combined with the constant presence of protein in my urine. They had decided that if I hadn't gone into labour on my own, then they would have to induce labour as soon as the pregnancy reached thirty-eight weeks. At that stage, they believed the baby's lungs would be strong enough for him to breathe on his own. I was still in quite a lot of pain from the SPD; it seemed as though I had no control over my body below my pelvis. This made me very anxious about my ability to push the baby out, although I was determined that I would be able to.

We spent the next few days anxiously waiting for the signs that the baby was ready to come out. This was not to be the case, however. I thought that my waters had broken, but the midwives didn't seem to be too concerned. I, however, was fearful that this might cause the baby to contract some form of life-threatening infection; I understood that this could be possible if there wasn't enough amniotic fluid around him.

The consultant took the decision to induce labour. I was moved to a private room, where I was given the injection on Monday, March 5. I honestly thought that with the induction I would have given birth the next day. I had never felt so much pain in my life before. I had been told that inducing labour pain would be quite painful, but I never imagined that it could be as painful as it was. While I was suffering this unbelievable amount of pain, I was still affected by the SPD. Eight hours after being induced, almost nothing was happening; my cervix was practically still solid shut.

I remember the consultant commenting that, for a woman who had miscarried at twenty weeks' gestation, it was remarkable that the cervix was still showing no sign of opening such a long time after being induced. The midwives started doing four-hourly checks, which felt like an eternity for me, given the amount of pain I was feeling.

Things continued like this for the next two and half days, until I was dilated to about eight centimetres and was taken to the delivery suite. Due to the presence of the large fibroid and the pre-eclampsia, I was prepared in advance to be taken to theatre as a precaution, in case a problem developed during delivery. I was also given an epidural to ease the pain from the induction and the SPD.

This made pushing extremely difficult as, after a while, I had no feeling below my pelvis, and wasn't able to tell when the pains became stronger. I pushed almost continuously for about an hour and a half before there was any sign of Michael Jr. It was very reassuring, though, that all this time he was being monitored on the cardiotocography (CTG) machine.

Michael was my cheerleader, encouraging me along and giving jokes and making me smile. There was a happy spirit in that delivery suite. At about three and half hours, Michael Jr was born. When he came out, he didn't start crying straightaway and, in fact, he sounded as if he was coughing or gasping for breath. "What's happened to my baby?" I asked. The midwife gave him two slaps on the side of his bottom, then he started to cry. "He is fine," she said. "He is going to be just fine." Minutes after cleaning him up, weighing him, taking some bloods and giving him the vitamin E injection, he was placed on my chest for us to bond.

He looked beautiful.

I used to hear stories about women in Jamaica; the first thing they did was to check the number of fingers and toes their newborn had. I didn't need to do this, as a student midwife duly did this for me. He looked very normal and that made him my perfect little boy. Was he the spitting image of his dad? No, I didn't think so, but no one could wipe the smile off Michael's face, as he was beaming from ear to ear. Moments later, he was on the phone to close friends and family, including my relieved mother in Jamaica.

One of the midwives commented that she had seen a few newborn babies in her time, and that MJ was one of the most beautiful babies she had ever seen.

This was a moment I would never forget, the moment when I realised my dream of becoming a mother. I was thankful to the Lord for His faithfulness to me in honouring His Word. It didn't matter how trivial such an achievement was to other people; for me, it was a victory over infertility. It was a victory over the shame and rejection that I had felt when I lost Hope. I had been restored.

I am aware that some people may have the view that women experience miscarriages all the time, but show me a woman who has lost her baby and is happy about it. To me, it is something that affects you deeply, but you have to decide how you want to deal with it: whether you allow it to consume you, or whether you use it as a motivation to appreciate that being a mother is indeed a privilege, and to appreciate that our children should be given the love and attention that they deserve.

My encounter with Salisbury District Hospital was an extremely sad one. It started when I was about six to seven weeks pregnant and I had arrived at A&E with fibroid pains. The doctor who saw me categorically said I was six weeks pregnant, then questioned whether I was really pregnant or not. Perhaps I should have known then that this was an indication of how I was going to be treated. In my opinion, had I been given the basic care in the hospital, they would have realised that I was in labour, and that I was losing my baby.

The consultant in Bristol had said that they would allow me to miscarry if necessary, but they had put everything in place to monitor me and the baby throughout the course of the pregnancy, even though

I hadn't expected to be pregnant at this stage. They didn't treat the life of my child like a lottery; if he lived that would have been OK, or if he had died they wouldn't have minded either.

21

It didn't take very long for the rigours of motherhood to set in. After giving birth, I returned to a ward with three other mothers. I initially told the midwives that I wanted to breastfeed my baby but, for some reason, Michael Jr just wasn't latching on. I became exasperated, as he was losing far more weight than was acceptable for a new-born. He was already smaller than the midwives had anticipated; they had expected him to be much heavier due to the gestational diabetes. In fact, his birth weight was only five pounds seven ounces. It seemed as though his weight had been affected by the pre-eclampsia.

Although I had explained that the baby was not taking the breast, I was still being pressured to persist, even though I expressed the desire to have him take the bottle. It seemed as though I was the only mother being pressured to breastfeed while other mothers were happily bottling feeding their babies. I noticed that this pressure was affecting my mental health, and it seemed that I was once again relapsing mentally. Michael Jr was a very good baby, and hardly cried at all; however, there was a woman who spent very little time with her baby. She was often away from her bed, having a smoke even at nights, and her baby would be left crying for long periods. At one point, she was reprimanded by the ward sister.

I believe it was the third night after Michael Jr was born. He was not taking the breast, and I was tired and frustrated. I rang Michael and he came to the hospital before seven that morning. He wasn't permitted to come onto the ward, so I wheeled the baby in his little cot to see him outside the ward. He gave me tremendous comfort and told me to convey to the midwives that I categorically wanted the baby to be bottle-fed as well as breastfed. Michael Jr then became stronger by the hour, and I was much happier. He was found to be jaundiced, however, because he hadn't been getting enough fluids to flush his system. I had to spend an additional week in hospital for this to clear up, after he was placed in an incubator under lights.

Michael Jr and I were discharged from hospital ten days after his birth. This was a very exciting time for us, but we had our first hiccup on the way home. Michael had not practised how to securely lock the car seat, and the hospital's policy was that the baby needed to be securely in the seat before we were allowed to leave. We were at the entrance of the hospital for about ten minutes (which seemed more like ten hours) with Michael frantically trying every way of properly securing this seat. The health care assistant was quietly standing by, looking bemused as my husband worked himself up to a frenzy. Thankfully MJ was sound asleep.

We were parked at the entrance of the hospital blocking the ambulance bay, which added even more pressure, when finally we heard a loud 'click'. This was a welcome relief; the baby was safely in. Michael had worked up a little sweat, but he jumped into the car, breaking into a smile. "Sorry about that, darling," he said to me, as he carefully drove out of the hospital premises. I sat in the back seat, staring adoringly at our baby. We drove along the M32 motorway, heading out of Bristol. It wasn't five minutes into the journey home, when we had to stop at a supermarket to get some supplies. I sat patiently while Michael got some more nappies and the formula milk that MJ seemed to favour while in hospital, and moments later we were on our way home.

My main priority was to make sure that the baby continued to increase in weight, so I had to make sure that young Michael was taking his bottle on a regular basis. He was quite tiny at birth, and had lost some weight due to the feeding issues that I had experienced while in hospital. I tried my best to put my motherly skills to work. Michael and I worked out a strategy for feeding. He suggested that while he was on the two weeks' paternity leave, he would do most of the care of the baby, so that I could recover properly. In addition, when he returned to work, he would take care of the baby from the time he arrived home until about 11.00 pm. The great thing was that Michael Jr slept perfectly through the nights most nights. In fact, I became concerned about this and rang my mother to ask if I should wake him up for a feed during the night. She assured me we would have known if he was hungry, as he would have woken up and cried.

For the most part, my life was in a happy place. I still missed Hope, but the raw sense of loss was slowly dissipating. I encouraged myself in the knowledge that if the Lord had wanted a different outcome, then that would have been the case.

I was very conscious that Michael and I were very close before Michael Jr came along, and so I was careful not to neglect him too much. At one point, though, I realised that I had been. MJ was quite a tiny baby, and I fed him quite regularly in order to increase his weight. I believe I became over-protective of him, so much so that Michael started to complain that he wasn't being allowed to care for him in the way he wanted to, as I would always be giving him instructions about what to do.

I quickly discovered that the transition from being a couple to becoming a family was not as easy as I had anticipated; there were challenges that could potentially affect how we related to each other. The changes in our lives were quite significant caring for this little person; everything took a little longer to do. Even going out was a challenge, as we found that it took far more time to get ready, and it took us a while to adjust to these little delays.

I believed one of the strongest assets of our marriage relationship was our friendship and, as any good friends should do whenever there is a problem, Michael and I quickly identified the challenges and had continuous dialogue about them. We didn't want the changes to affect our relationship and to diminish the joy of parenthood, so we listened to each other and compromised as much as we could. Did we achieve perfection? No, far from it, but we worked hard to plant the seeds in building a close and loving family.

22

Michael Jr was growing nicely. He met all his growth and development targets and, thankfully, he had no medical problems. Michael and I combined well in caring for him.

Prior to going on maternity leave, I had to submit a posting preference indicating the regiments where I would like to work after maternity leave. The form stipulated that I indicated three locations in preference order. I had specified that I would like to return to my current unit at Colerne; my mental health had improved along with my productivity and working relationship with my colleagues. I had also put Warminster and Chepstow as my second and third choices, respectively.

Unfortunately, I received a phone call from my caseworker at the Personnel Unit to inform me that my request to return to Colerne had been refused on the grounds that I had taken every opportunity to go off sick. I guess they were referring to my ill health when I was pregnant. At no time did I ever pretend to be ill. I am sure there is no way I could have pretended to have Symphysis Pubis Dysfunction, pre-eclampsia, gestational diabetes or even the postnatal depression I'd experienced after the loss of my baby, Hope.

I was assured by the caseworker, however, that I had the option to apply to be transferred to other units, as the Army normally granted requests from soldiers returning from maternity leave. I decided that, although this location was very convenient for

Michael to attend work in Bristol and we could still be close to church, I would apply to another regiment in the Chippenham area.

I resubmitted a new posting preference to that effect, and I was accepted at 9th Supply Regiment Royal Logistics Corps. I was quite happy about this, as it afforded me an opportunity of a reasonably fresh start, after having my child and all that I had previously been through.

I only had a few more weeks left on maternity leave and I had to try to make the most of it, spending quality time with my newborn and adjusting to being both a mother and wife.

My maternity leave went swiftly by, and I started to make preparations to return to work. While on maternity leave, I had been temporarily posted to Y-List, the section of the Army personnel unit in Glasgow. When the time came, I submitted the necessary paperwork to Y-List, who arranged the move.

The removal guys packed and delivered our effects to our new home. Since we were moving only fifteen minutes from where we lived previously, Michael and I went for the house (Army quarters) to be handed over to us.

On arrival, the representative from Defence Housing was already there, but the first thing we noticed was a fierce stench emanating from inside the property. The representative tried to fob off the smell, trying to persuade us that it would dissipate, and suggested that we should accept it as it had been cleaned prior to our arrival. However, we were secretly told by an agent (also with the Defence Housing) that we should not accept the property in the state it was in.

The smell was like a mixture of dog urine and dog hair. There was evidence of dog hair still in the carpet in the living and dining rooms. The smell was not as evident upstairs, but there was no way we were going to accept the property in such a state, especially with our young baby. The Defence Housing representative hurriedly arranged for the carpet to be deep-cleaned and gave us the commitment that it would be replaced as soon as possible. We thought that this was a reasonable solution, and so accepted the property.

Michael and I were now faced with the dilemma of whether to send Michael Jr to the crèche on camp or to have another mother on camp look after him while we were at work. The difficulty with the latter was that, since we had only recently moved to the regiment, it wasn't as easy to find someone whom we trusted to look after our child, and the option to take him to crèche would prove to be very expensive. It would have cost approximately £980.00 per month, and only if I kept to a strict nine to five daily time schedule. This was far too expensive for us, so we opted to have my sister come down from the Midlands to care for MJ during the week. This was a very good solution for him to be cared for by his aunt. This solution put my mind at ease, and allowed me to be more focused on my work.

I started preparing to return to work and improving my fitness, by walking for up to an hour every day, depending on how I was feeling, pushing MJ in his pushchair around the camp. After my work medical, I was given the all clear to return to work.

I went back to work, very enthusiastic about my job. I was assigned to work as junior clerk with a sergeant in a squadron. I tried as usual to apply myself in carrying out my tasks to the best of my ability and skill, utilising my knowledge base as a clerk. I was more than eager to learn new things, as I was aware that this would make me more efficient in performing my job. Although I knew that maternity leave was mandatory by law, I was cognisant of the fact that I had been ill a lot during the pregnancy, and was also aware that I had been out of the loop, so to speak, for approximately six months, and wanted to get back into the flow of things almost straightaway. So I tried my hardest to prove myself to my superiors and colleagues. I found that I wasn't too rusty but needed to catch up in a few areas. I viewed this as a challenge and worked till late some evenings in order to catch up.

Approximately eight weeks after returning to work, I noticed that I had some difficulty fitting into my uniform. I found this a bit strange, as these were new uniforms that I had received due to the obvious weight gain from the pregnancy. I simply thought that I had been eating too much, and thought nothing more of it.

However, this was becoming an issue I could no longer afford to ignore. Could I be pregnant again? I asked myself. No, not at all, I told myself, but there was this little voice in my head that kept saying to me, 'Go and have a pregnancy test done.' I argued with myself that I would feel very guilty if this had happened. What would they say at work? How would I cope with being ill? I had only just come from a regiment that had refused to take me back because of pregnancy-related illnesses. I was a thirty-one-year-old married woman, I assured myself, who would just be having my second child, but the reality was that I was a female soldier in a very male-dominated environment. How on earth was I going to survive this? It was a frightening prospect.

At this stage, I hadn't even confirmed that I was pregnant again, but I had started to have some feelings similar to what I had experienced the previous two times.

I had a very good relationship with the caseworker at Y-List, who I asked for advice. She suggested that I should not worry about individuals at work, irrespective of rank. She further added that it was the responsibility of the managers to look after the welfare of all soldiers – including those who were pregnant.

This support gave me a greater level of confidence to face my managers, and I booked an appointment with the doctor. She did a pregnancy test and, yes, it was positive. I was pregnant again, but I wasn't sure if I was happy; I was somewhat happy but still felt a burden of guilt. Why did I feel this way? I felt that I had a responsibility to my job, and furthermore, Michael Jr was just four months at that time. I was concerned about the care and attention I would be able to give to him, especially with the prospect perhaps developing difficulties in pregnancy again, some of which I still had not fully recovered from. Nonetheless, I was hoping for a girl. Ever since I'd lost my daughter, Hope, I so much desired to have another girl, just to see what she would look like, and to have a mother and daughter relationship.

I informed Michael over the phone about our good news. He, too, was overjoyed, but straightaway expressed concern about what the reaction would be at work.

23

To my pleasant surprise, however, the regiment was quite supportive at the news. Due to the multiplicity of medical complications I had experienced with the previous pregnancies, the doctor reduced my hours, which meant that I worked from 08.00 to 13.30, Monday to Friday. I was also to be excluded from being duty clerk.

I was grateful for this support; I worked as hard as I could during these shortened hours at work. The doctor informed me that the Detachment stated that they wanted someone 'fit and well' to work in the squadron. They suggested that I could go sick for the duration of the pregnancy, prior to going on maternity leave.

Personally, I felt as if I owed the Army to be at work, and didn't want to take the option of going on sick leave. The doctor, however, stated that although she understood my position, she suggested that I should not fight this proposal, and should take up the offer of going off sick. After hearing this from the doctor, I reluctantly decided to go on sick leave. Despite the potential difficulties of falling pregnant again so soon, I had been determined to be at work.

This meant that I was, once again, transferred under the care of Y-List much sooner than originally anticipated. At this stage, I was just past the twenty-week point in the pregnancy.

The antenatal care was once again led by the proficient consultant at St Michael's Hospital in

Bristol. Even though I had no concerns whatsoever about having another miscarriage, the medical team at the hospital recommended that I had the regular fortnightly scans, in order to see what was happening with the cervix.

My main worry with this pregnancy was, however, the pre-eclampsia. This time it was much worse than before. I started having increased blood pressure levels from an early stage in the pregnancy.

We found out the sex of the baby when we went for the scan at twenty weeks. We were having a girl. I felt very blessed indeed that my heart's desire of having a girl had been granted by the Lord. Now I felt that my family would be complete.

I noticed that the pain from the fibroid was not as intense as before. It was certainly still there, and I tried my best to deal with the pain as best I could. At about twenty-three weeks, I felt as if the baby had turned across my stomach. I shared this concern with the midwife at the Green Ways maternity centre in Chippenham, who checked and confirmed that the baby was transverse.

About a week later, I felt as if the baby had turned again, this time I felt as if her feet were in my groin area. I again shared this with the midwife, who confirmed that she was a small baby with enough space inside my womb so she could turn all the time. The midwife further assured me that, based on her experience, the baby would turn again to the normal position by the time she was due to be born.

Michael and I were almost very sure that this would not be the case. We thought that she was going to remain in this breached position, because she was competing with the large fibroid in the womb.

As the weeks progressed, the discomfort from the baby being breached increased; at times I literally felt as though I was going to die. It was as if her head was constantly resting against my lungs, making it difficult for me to breathe. Lying down was particularly terrible for me. I can remember one night I woke in a state of panic, as if gasping for breath. On the occasions when this happened, I felt that I wouldn't make it through the pregnancy.

In my opinion, the doctors at St Michael's Hospital did not seem too perturbed about my discomfort. They said that there was enough time for the baby to turn in time for her birth.

While this was happening, Michael and I had to agree on the name for the baby. Since our son was named Michael Jr, we agreed that I would come up with the name of our little girl. It didn't take too long for me to come up with the name Makayla, which meant "Who is like our God?" The Lord had been so faithful to Michael and me, we certainly wanted to mark her life with a name that represented our thanks to Jehovah God.

The SPD started to get worse as the pregnancy progressed. In addition, the breached baby was causing me to become more and more anxious each time she stretched her legs and pushed her head onto my lungs. The most serious concern to me, however, was the pre-eclampsia. It is said that pre-eclampsia normally improves by the second pregnancy in most women, but in my situation it seemed to be certainly getting worse by the day.

The consultant and her team decided that they would take me into hospital for the remainder of the pregnancy, in order to monitor me closely. At this point, I was twenty-nine weeks pregnant. They were particularly concerned with the severity of the pre-eclampsia and it would be far better to care for me in hospital. Had I remained at home, they felt I would exert myself with the usual activities of being a wife and mother of a young child, which would have exacerbated the condition.

The plan was again to see how far I could cope with the pregnancy, with a caesarean section scheduled at thirty-eight weeks. I dreaded the prospect of being hospital for that length of time, but was determined to make whatever sacrifice necessary to take this little girl home.

To live in a confined space surrounded by sick, pregnant women was daunting, to say the least. The first couple of days were OK, but then I started missing my boys and the comfort of my home. Michael would take MJ to visit every day, but still I felt that my baby was growing away from me. I remember one evening he said in his tiny voice, "I'm ready, daddy." I felt very sad and couldn't hold back the tears, when he held his father's hand and headed towards the exit, and said "Bye, mummy," waving his arms as he went. Although I was extremely sad, I was comforted that he was happy being with his dad, which gave me peace of mind so I could concentrate on myself and the pregnancy.

I spent a lot of time reading and watching daytime television, and naturally I spent a significant number of minutes on the phone with my boys. At the time, there were no unlimited mobile phone bundles, so my phone bill was very high.

There were other long-term patients like me, as well as those who came and went on numerous occasions. There was a woman who was about thirty-five, who fell into the latter category. We chatted whenever we met in the lounge or at lunch. She had told me that she and her husband had been trying for a child for nearly ten years, but she had only conceived by IVF and was having complications with the pregnancy. At the time, she was twenty-four weeks pregnant and lived in Weston-Super-Mare. Like me, she was referred to that hospital for antenatal care. Each time she was admitted for several days, then discharged and a few days later she was back again. She suffered with excessive bleeding in pregnancy.

She was quite teary most of the time. She had been trying naturally for such a long time and had only conceived via IVF, so she was desperately afraid that she might lose her child.

Another woman on the ward with me, who I think was forty-six years old, also suffered from pre-eclampsia, and this was her first pregnancy. Most of the time, we supported each other, but there were times we were all just fed up with being around several under-fed pregnant women. The lack of food on the hospital ward was the topic of conversation every day. Breakfast every morning was a tiny bowl of porridge or cereal, with toast. At no time were we given a full English or anything like that – not even a scrambled egg. The lunch room was full of hungry, pregnant women up to twenty minutes before lunch was due to be served, and many times we just sat there chatting and drinking tea. I found it funny to watch the actions of these women, some walking gingerly, swaying from side to side and holding onto their stomachs, while others would be taking tiny steps while holding their backs.

From what I observed, I had very little to eat compared with some of the other women, but the pre-eclampsia had caused me to put on loads of weight due to the water retention.

The weeks crept by at a very slow pace. I became very frustrated at having been in hospital for such a long time, and I missed being home with my family.

I was eventually allowed to go home for an hour one Saturday afternoon. Michael picked me up at 4.00 pm and should have taken me back by about 5.30 pm, but I maximised the opportunity to be at home and stayed until about 8.00 pm.

At thirty-six weeks, I became severely impatient. In my mind, the pregnancy was at the stage where the baby could be delivered, as I started to struggle even more with the effects of the pre-eclampsia, and the fact that she was still breached and pressing against my lungs became even more unbearable. It wasn't as if I was in my own space, and could be comforted by husband, or even enjoy the antics of my little son; I was stuck on a hospital ward.

Fair enough, the doctors were giving my baby the best chance of survival and, to a great extent, preserving my own life, but unfortunately the way I was feeling, I just couldn't see it that way. There many times I had arguments with the Obstetrics registrar, who ensured that I was kept totally in check.

Finally a date was set, as the doctors now felt that by the thirty-eighth week, the baby was now able to breathe unaided. They continued to give steroids in case the baby decided to make an early arrival.

A few weeks prior to being admitted to hospital, Michael and I had started the process of buying a house. Initially, we wanted to get a house in the Bristol area, but were deterred by not having the £35,000 deposit required by the developers. Although we were disappointed with not being able to buy this house, we soon switched location and got a good deal from the same developers in the West Midlands.

It was difficult for me to travel up to the Midlands for viewings and eventually to sign the legal documents. We had to go in person to the solicitor's office on one occasion, but all the other documents were sent to us through the post. Michael had to take the papers for me to sign, while I was still in hospital.

This was an important personal achievement for us. Michael was particularly determined to buy this house; he was an old-fashioned man, who strongly believed that it was important to have a home for his family to live in. He was determined to make sure that we didn't just depend on living in Army quarters indefinitely, and that we didn't have to live somewhere we didn't want to when the time came to leave the Army.

For me, personally, obtaining my own home was a far cry from the drama I had experienced as a child. Looking back to when I attended secondary school in Jamaica, I remember one evening I was on the bus, approaching my stop (which was located opposite our house) and, as I looked into my yard, I saw something that was disturbing. I honestly couldn't believe what I was seeing at first, and so I had to look again intently. "The roof is gone!" I gasped. Immediately, my throat became parched dry; I had to salivate to ensure that I didn't pass out. I felt a deep sense of shame, as I wondered to myself what could have happened.

I hurriedly crossed the road and burst through the gate. I went into the yard and realised that the majority of the roof had been taken off. I found my mother sitting in the doorway, with her left hand holding onto her cheek, looking very distressed with tears running down her face. "What happened, Mummy?" I asked curiously. She eventually told me that the landlord (who was a returning resident from England) had had the roof removed, due to the mounting rent arrears. I was devastated, but could not cry till much later in the evening. I felt as though my life was crumbling.

We all had to go into the one room that had been spared. We lived like this for approximately eight weeks, until we rented a house owned by one of my aunts.

After my family had moved into my aunt's house, we had to quit after about nine months. My aunt had had to return to this house because she had fallen on hard times, and had to sell the house she had moved to. They had a shop attached to the house, though, which they allowed us to occupy, and we lived there for approximately eighteen months.

Later, my mother and I went and located a piece of land not far from where we lived in the shop. I have no idea where my mother got the boards from, which made the little one room house but, at nights when the lights were turned on, you could see many revealing holes which perforated the entire building, and which we covered by pasting newspaper and magazines. Despite the many hardships I endured growing up, this inspired me to work hard to ensure that this type of drama would never happen to me again. I wanted to avoid these kinds of events affecting my children the way they had impacted my young life.

The day finally arrived for the C-section surgery to bring Makayla into the world. Naturally, I was feeling quite nervous, but trusted the Lord that everything would go to plan. I was up early and had nothing to eat. I waited for hours for them to take me down to theatre. All the doctors and nurses were quite reassuring about what was going to take place and, as usual, my husband was by my side. There was a great vibe in the operating theatre.

The surgery itself was a bit surreal. All I could feel was a tugging from my lower abdomen, and moments later my beautiful baby girl was placed onto my chest.

"Hello, it's mummy," I said. "Welcome to our family," staring at her face.

About an hour later, I was taken to the recovery ward, where Michael and I were joined by a couple friends. I was feeling numb, but was relieved that she had arrived safely. Another three hours elapsed before I was taken back to the ward.

Makayla and I spent the first night together without any issues at all. She ate and slept really well; the only thing was that I was restricted in handling her as I still had the catheter attached to me.

The next day, however, she was taken into the neonatal intensive care unit, where she spent a number of days. The doctor had some concerns about her blood. At one point, they were thinking of doing a full blood transfusion if her blood count had not improved, but fortunately this was not necessary.

While under antenatal care, one of the topics that the expectant mothers did not discuss at all was Downs Syndrome. When I went on the postnatal ward, however, everybody appeared relieved that their baby did not have the condition. There seemed to be a collective sigh of relief, and each mother expressed their own secret fear that their child could potentially have been born with the disorder.

After Makayla came out of the neonatal intensive care unit, I spent a further week in hospital before being discharged. One week after being discharged with my newborn, I went along with Michael to pick up the keys for our brand new house. Life was very good.

24

Securing the house was part of the plan that I'd had to leave the Army after giving birth to my second child. Michael and I had discussed that, although I was a clerk, having two young children thirteen months apart would be a difficult undertaking for a woman who had no relatives around to offer any support in caring for them. I hoped so much that I could have my mother around to give us support.

We decided to move into our home, which we did around the middle of May 2008, while I was still on my maternity leave. Army regulations stated that a soldier on maternity leave could give notice to leave the services while still on maternity leave. This was what I decided to do.

A few months after moving home, we went on holiday to Jamaica in order to introduce our children to our respective families over the Christmas season that year. We had a grand time in the sun.

While I was in Jamaica on the holiday, however, I struggled with the decision whether to leave the Army. I loved my job, and I could not just walk away from it like that. After returning to the UK, I decided that I would return to work.

The idea I had was either to get a posting in the Midlands area, where I could travel from my home to work or the less favourable of the two options was to return to the regiment in the South West and return home on weekends.

I am not sure what prompted the RAO, who I had not met before, to call me at my home. He mentioned something about returning to work in Chippenham, but I told him that I would like to be transferred to a regiment in the West Midlands area. I can't remember what exactly transpired during the conversation, but I can remember telling him that I was previously advised by my caseworker at Y-List that I should not be in direct contact with anyone from the regiment while I was on maternity leave. I was careful not to sound disrespectful, even though I was annoyed that he had rung me while I was on maternity leave. I am sure he knew that any contact should have been done via Y-List.

Two weeks later, I received a letter from the department that I was being transferred back to the unit in Chippenham. I was very disappointed, as I wanted so much to remain in the West Midlands area so that I could travel to work from my home.

In my mind, the RAO had had his way in getting me to return to the regiment. I tried to get the posting changed, but to no avail. I therefore had to move my family back down to the South West. We moved back in January 2009, and I returned to work about two weeks afterwards.

Prior to coming off maternity leave, I had a conversation with the chief clerk about changing my cap badge from clerk to chef. He was not impressed with the idea, however. He said I should not worry, and that they would take care of me because they knew I'd had a difficult time in the Army up to that stage. He informed me that they would get me to attend in-house training courses to rebuild my current skill levels. It was very reassuring to hear this coming from the chief clerk as, to date, I had never experienced this level of support from any of my previous managers in the Army.

I must admit, I was sceptical of his assurances and his support, and told myself that only time would tell if he was genuine in what he'd said. This chief clerk, the RAO and Det Commander, as well as all the other members of the AGC (SPS) were wonderful in their support towards me. For the first time since I'd joined Army, it was a joy to turn up for work in the mornings.

I was placed in a squadron where the senior clerk was a Jamaican guy. It was a joy working with him; in many ways, Jermaine and I worked as a team to achieve our goals and targets, and we did outstandingly well looking out for each other.

The camaraderie in this team of people was brilliant, and we had many social events within the Det that we enjoyed, which involved our respective families.

This level of camaraderie was not to last for too long, however, and, to my detriment, within an eight-month period almost all the staff, who worked in the Det at that time, were posted away, due the Army's staff rotation system.

What I feared would happen seemed to become reality, as many of the new people who came, started to exercise the authority of the superior rank, and ensured that I knew my place as a private. In many instances, my self-confidence had been crushed, and I felt a level of pressure on the job that I had experienced at the 1 Black Watch and 21 Signal Regiments.

This felt both scary and humiliating; I realised that I was now frequently being asked how long I had been in the Army and whether I had always been a clerk.

I had been trying relentlessly to prove myself to them, and to show that I was capable of carrying out my tasks both effectively and efficiently. So when the time finally came for me to go and do my Class 1 course, I was determined to go and do well.

It was a residential course, located at the AGC Training School in Winchester. I did the course, which, a few years earlier, would have been a six-week course had now been compressed into a two-week course with exams at the end. I passed some the modules, but had to do a couple re-sits, which was quite a common occurrence for others on the course. I knew my limitations and so returned to class in the evenings, along with a few others, not only to practise what I had learnt but also to give me the edge in grasping what had been taught.

I was struck by the RAO's reaction when I returned to work and informed him that I had passed the course. "You passed!" he exclaimed. "Yes, sir," I replied. "Did you really pass Private Hall?" He asked, seemingly genuinely shocked. I was hurt by his reaction, as I had never seen him react in that way to anybody else. It was as if he hadn't expected me to pass but, thank God, I did. I believed if I hadn't passed, this would surely have been used against me at every opportunity as grounds to force me out of my job.

The relationship I had with the newer members of the Det was uncomfortable, to say the least. I started to feel resented and alienated. Many times, I felt that I was being put under intense pressure, and none of the senior clerks assisted in any area of the job I could not deal with by myself, while others at the same level were treated differently, in my opinion. On one occasion, another junior clerk made a massive error in not moving and tracking the Commanding

Officer properly. The guy who did this was promoted soon afterwards, without even having to complete the Class 1 course that I had been ridiculed for passing. This course was normally the benchmark used to promote clerks to the rank of lance corporal, yet he had been promoted without it.

In my opinion, if I had committed this error, there most certainly would have been severe repercussions.

I noticed that I started having flu-related illnesses quite a lot, and felt as though I was always very tired. I also started to suffer from lack of sleep. My attitude was that the medical doctors were there to assist in getting me better, so I went to the medical centre for help.

As soon as I had recovered from one thing, it seemed as if I was suffering from another. The fibroid started acting up and my stomach would be painfully swollen for days, for example. I also had headaches that I just could not shift at all. This was not a happy time. Anyway, the Christmas break came, and I felt that I could use this time to get better so I could be stronger at work in the New Year 2010.

25

My family and I had a quiet and peaceful Christmas, especially the children. We had to replace a number of balls and lights destroyed by Makayla, but it was all fun. I went to work in the New Year, optimistic with the hope that things would get better.

The RAO had left, and was replaced by an older man. This meant that I was one of the only two people left from the team that I had seen after returning from maternity leave.

Things remained pretty much the same, but I just stayed by myself. I did what I had to do, but did not ask anyone in the Det for any assistance in dealing with problem matters. Instead, I rang my friend Shelley, who was now posted in another part of the country, or Jermaine, now working in Scotland, and I got by.

I only felt comfortable when I was out of my office and interacting with the African and fellow Caribbean soldiers on camp.

The constant pressure had led to me having low feelings, similar to how I felt when I lost the baby, but in a slightly different way. I found it very difficult to sleep at nights, and became extremely nervous whenever I arrived at the gate at work. I would experience tummy aches and butterflies. I complained on more than one occasion both to the sergeant major in the squadron and to his counterpart in the AGC Det. This resulted in an apology from him, but his behaviour still continued.

My relationship with the regiment seemed to hit an all-time low after the car I was travelling in ran off the road into a ditch. This happened just by the disused airfield in Hullavington, very close to where we lived.

It was a Monday afternoon, when I was on my way home for lunch, having been picked up by one of my friends. As the car approached the corner, it started to skid and ended up on its side, with me in the passenger seat, suspended in the air. Michael was at home, and I was able to call him and he swiftly drove to where we were.

The practice manager for the medical centre, who was a sergeant, was also going home for lunch and saw us in the state we were, but he did nothing to help except to tell Michael to call the emergency services, which he did.

The fire crew came and suggested that they would have to cut the car to release us, but my friend started to cry, saying that she didn't want her car to be destroyed. She told them that she would walk out and did so, despite being advised not to do that. They made it clear that they were not going to risk injury in having me freed, and that they would have to cut off the top and the car doors. I was taken by ambulance to hospital, but was discharged several hours later and given a letter to take to the medical officer.

The next day, I turned up at the medical centre to see the doctor. Just as I was about to speak to the receptionist, I was attacked by the said sergeant, who had been present at the scene of the accident and had left to go and have his lunch rather than stay and help us. "You could have walked out the car, couldn't you?" he said in an aggressive tone of voice. "You didn't have to call the ambulance, did you? I told you that I could get you out, but you were afraid, weren't you?" he continued ranting. I couldn't believe what was happening, I was so shocked at his tirade that I froze for a few seconds, not knowing how to respond. "No, you did not say that. You told Michael to call the ambulance and even told him to go and get a sheet to cover me," I eventually responded.

Michael was incensed at how this guy was speaking to me. Michael then asked me, "Is this the way they talk to you?" I felt as if I wanted to sink through the floor. "I'd rather you came out," he continued.

"You are a liar," Michael said to this sergeant. "I was there when you arrived, and that is not what you said," Michael added. He began to shout and swear at Michael, who calmly told him not to swear at him, but that he should swear at his wife and dogs at his home.

I was so ashamed at being spoken to like this in the presence of my husband. I didn't want Michael to see this side of the Army, and how they shouted and swore at us. At this point, I didn't feel like I wanted to even see the doctor, but my husband convinced me that I shouldn't allow the sergeant to prevent me from receiving care.

I saw a civilian doctor, who prescribed painkillers and signed me off work for three days.

I returned to work on the Friday. It seemed that this sergeant had spread malicious and wicked lies around the camp, suggesting that I had pretended to be injured in the accident, when I was not. Just because my friend had walked out of the car, meant that I, too, should have just walked out as well. I genuinely wanted to do that, especially when I saw her getting out. I was fearful of what the repercussions could have been, and this is exactly what happened. I had begged the ambulance crew to let me walk out of the car as well, but they were adamant that the way I was positioned in the car meant that they would not allow me to walk.

Things gradually got to the stage where my work was put under intense scrutiny, and life and work reached an all time low.

At first, I felt hurt that people were telling me I was no good and that I was lazy. I also felt rejected and victimised, but I was adamant that I would fight them. I had no one to turn to; I was on my own as a private, feeling marginalised and demoralised, but I decided that I was not giving them the joy of resigning from my job. I had worked hard to get into this position, and asked myself why should I allow myself to be forced out of my job? Like all of them I, too, had a family to look after and a mortgage to pay.

I felt that my mental health had started to deteriorate. I was having difficulty sleeping; I had no appetite and practically no interest in my family at all. Michael was my only source of support, and encouraged me to go and see the doctor. I was very reluctant to do this because of the fear that I would be poorly treated, especially following the previous incident with the practice manager.

I knew that I was relapsing into depression once again. Michael went ahead and bought some Kalms tablets for me. These are herbal tablets that are meant to keep you calm in times of stress.

I started remembering all the treatment that I had received at the other regiments, and started to question why was this always happening to me? Was it my personality, my Christianity, or my upbringing? I started to ask, 'Why?' I kept beating myself up, saying that I should have joined the chefs or suppliers; this, I concluded, was the reason why I wanted to be transferred.

Michael eventually convinced me to go to the medical centre. He pointed out that he didn't want me to return to how I was before, because he was happy with the progress I had made in getting over the loss of the baby. He also mentioned that I was withdrawn from the family, and that my eyes were looking 'wild'. I wept bitterly, because I knew what was happening in my head, but I had no idea that he had observed these emotional and physical changes too.

At this point, I longed so much to be with my mother; I missed her so much. I told Michael to take me home to Jamaica. He assured me that the Lord would take care of me, while he would fast and pray for a favourable resolution.

Unfortunately, the Kalms that my husband had bought were not helping me at all, so I decided to go to the medical centre to get proper medical care from the doctor. I didn't want to go back to that dark and scary place again.

The doctor on duty that day was an elderly ex-Army officer. As I greeted him and was about to sit down, he asked, "What now?" I was mortified at this question and tone of voice. I said, "Sir, I need your help." By this time, tears were just flowing down my cheeks. "I am depressed, and I have been through depression before in 2005, after the loss of my pregnancy at twenty weeks," I continued. He then said that I had been to the medical centre over eighty-nine times in the past year, and only an eighty-year-old woman would go to the doctor that number of times and I was only thirty-four. He went on to add that he was an older person, and he had only visited the doctor about five times a year.

He asked me, "What do you think your managers would think about you going to the doctor so many times?"

"No, sir. I have not been to the medical centre that number of times," I calmly replied. "Probably what you are seeing was when I was pregnant, with a very difficult pregnancy," I continued.

"And you even went on maternity leave," he said in a derogatory tone of voice, with his eyebrows firmly knitted together.

There is absolutely no way I would have been allowed to go to the medical centre that number of times while at work. This would have meant that I had gone to the doctor an average of nearly 7.5 times per month, including the holiday periods.

However, I began telling him about the stress that I was experiencing at work, and how it was causing me to feel. I explained that I was not sleeping either. He then asked if I had gone to see my managers, to which I replied that I had, but there had been no change.

He then said to me, "Clearly, you are not happy in your job. Why don't you change your cap badge?" I replied that I couldn't, because I now had cold injury, and no other cap badge would accept me. He mentioned that I would not be deployable, and I agreed.

I honestly didn't expect this level of argument and lack of support from the doctor, and by this time, my mind was even more all over the place. I then said to him, "Sir, is it because I am Black?" Before I could even finish the statement, he jumped in sternly, "Don't draw any race card inside here." He then asked, "Where are you from?" I replied, "Jamaica, sir." By this time, I was feeling more exhausted, even more ill, and more humiliated than when I'd started the consultation.

He asked, "Do you have any friends on camp?" But before I could even answer this question, he added, "There are a lot of Commonwealth soldiers and Jamaicans on camp. You are supposed to be happy, aren't you?" By then, I was ready to get up and leave, as it was clear that he was not going to help me. He had shown no interest in my mental illness, and in nothing relating to how I was feeling.

He didn't think it was a medical problem but a work problem, and suggested I go back to my managers, or go and speak to the welfare officer. I cried through the remainder of the consultation, and he said that because I was crying so much, he was giving me one day off to 'get myself together'. I told him that I did not want the day off but he insisted, and I eventually agreed. I went straight to the welfare officer before heading home.

I was an absolute mess when I got home. It felt as if I had just completed a twelve-round boxing match with a heavyweight boxer. I was tired and felt pain in my joints. I had a headache and I could neither eat nor sleep, as the events of the day just kept repeating in my head over and over again.

Michael was very concerned about me, and suggested that I return to see the doctor in the morning. He knew I was not pretending to be ill, and didn't want me to go back into depression. He suggested that I needed some anti-depressants to get me settled so that I could cope at work, as well as to be able to carry out my normal family duties. Michael emphasised that if I was feeling mentally ill, the doctor was the person that I should go to for medical help.

I was so afraid to encounter this doctor again, so Michael decided to accompany me to the consultation. On entering the room, Michael humbly explained to him that it was with great trepidation that I was back, and this was the reason he had come to support me.

Michael reiterated that I had suffered a miscarriage under extremely difficult circumstances, which had resulted in me developing postnatal depression. It seemed as if I was displaying the same symptoms as before. Michael also added that I had shared with him that I wanted to "do away with myself". The doctor then asked in an aggressive tone, "Do you have any thoughts of hurting the children?" For some reason, I couldn't answer this question. I began to cry and became very angry with him. How dare he ask me if I wanted to hurt my children! I guess that, as a doctor, he had the right to ask these questions. What troubled me, however, was the rigid tone in which he was addressing me. I was almost at my lowest ebb, and had expected a medical doctor to be a source of support, irrespective of the fact that I was a soldier.

"You are not answering, so that is a Yes? Yes?" he continued, to my amazement.

"No, sir," I replied.

Michael then said to him, "I know my wife, and I know when she is ill. Could you prescribe an anti-depressant – even one as low as 5mg – to settle her down? She has been treated with anti-depressants before."

He responded by saying that he didn't think that I was depressed. It was out of his hands, and he was going to contact the DCMH at RAF Brize Norton for an assessment. They would know if I was depressed or not. He further added that he would contact the relevant authorities about the children, as well as the managers and the regiment's padre.

I was concerned and thought to myself, 'What is happening to me?' as I feared that this man would have caused the authorities to take my children away from me. At this point, I felt even more ill; I thought, 'This is it, now I am getting mad.'

I was desperately determined to get help, as I was feeling similar to how I felt when I suffered the miscarriage with Hope. So Michael accompanied me once more to see the doctor the next morning, and this time we took the children along with us.

We waited for a considerable amount of time before the doctor let us in. When we went in, the doctor greeted us and introduced us to the military doctor. He stated that, since he was not in uniform, he had brought this officer to reinforce what he was telling me.

Michael spoke to the other doctor about me being depressed because of the treatment I was receiving at work. He agreed that patients can become depressed due to stress at work, but said I did not fall into this category. The original doctor then said that he would end the consultation, as it wasn't me doing the talking and I had to go to work, because at the moment I had gone AWOL.

Michael then informed them that he would be making a complaint regarding the doctor's unprofessional conduct.

I decided that I was not going to go to work in the state I was in, and that I would be willing to go to Colchester prison. (This is where the Army prison is located.) Michael said that he didn't want me to go AWOL, as this would upset the children's lives, so he suggested that I speak directly to the DCMH at RAF Brize Norton.

Initially I told Michael that I wasn't going to call them, as all of them (military doctors) were the same. I felt as though the GP at the medical centre would have rung and told a lot of lies about me.

I later decided to call the DCMH, because I knew if I hadn't, I would have been deemed to have gone AWOL.

I was angry with this doctor and his terrible, unjustified attitude towards me. I was surprised that a medical professional, whom I should turn to for help in a situation such as mine, was treating me like I was some kind of pariah. This was Britain in the twenty-first century, and I was determined that I wasn't going to accept that type of treatment from anyone. Nothing would cause me to return to the dark place of depression again. This time, I knew what was happening to me. It was not like the first time, when I didn't understand what was happening. Back then, I promised myself that if this should happen to me again, then I would seek professional help at the earliest opportunity. I wasn't allowing these individuals, regardless of who they were, to prevent me from getting the help I needed. I wanted to be well enough to take care of my family and myself, especially in the years after leaving the Army.

I mustered up the courage and rang the number at the DCMH at RAF Brize Norton. The receptionist answered, and I began to tell her what had been happening to me, crying all the time I was talking to her. I wasn't sure if they had been told about me beforehand, but she told me to hold the line, as she was going to transfer me to a psychiatrist.

The doctor confirmed that he had been contacted about me earlier. He then asked what had been happening. I didn't trust him at first – and made that clear to him – but I went on to explain what I had been experiencing with the Detachment, as well the ex-Army officer who had now become the GP at the medical centre.

I was crying hysterically while speaking to him, and he said I should come and see him at RAF Brize Norton immediately.

From where we lived, it would take just over an hour's drive to get to the airbase located in Oxfordshire. Since we didn't have anyone to look after the children for us, we had to take them along as well. When we arrived, Michael stayed in the waiting room with the children, while I went in to see the doctor.

I spent over an hour explaining what had been happening to me. I pointed out the fact that I had experienced depression before, and that the GP had been denying that I was ill. In an effort to seek medical help for this condition, this was why I had come to see him.

He signed me off work for a week, and prescribed a course of anti-depressants. He advised me that I should return to my GP before the week was over, in order for my condition to be reviewed.

26

I spent the next few days reflecting on what had been happening to me. For the most part, I kept asking 'Why?' Michael and I just could not understand why this was happening to us. All I had wanted was to receive the necessary care to prevent my mental health from deteriorating to the point where I wasn't able to cope with taking care of my children.

It was bad enough to have been mistreated by my work colleagues, but the main shock to the system was the treatment by the doctor. I was in utter disbelief that a doctor could have treated his patient in the way I had been. I believed that this further affected my mental health.

I decided that, despite the way I was being treated by these people, I was determined to look after myself. Since I had been signed off by the psychiatrist, I made sure I returned to the medical centre for a review before the week had elapsed.

I saw a different doctor at the medical centre on this occasion; she was covering for the senior medical officer who was away on sick leave.

She informed me that she had received a letter from the psychiatrist, stating that I needed to de-stress, but she hadn't been told about that. Again, I had to fight with another doctor at the medical centre; it was obvious that this wasn't going to be an easy time for me. She went on to undermine the qualification of the psychiatrist who had given me the week off, stating that he was a junior.

I requested to work part-time, but she made it clear that there was 'no part-time' in the Army. I needed to consider my job, as they would throw me out the Army. She then suggested that I went to see the RAO as he was not an ogre.

She didn't ask me how I was feeling or anything relating to my health.

I returned to work, and went straight to see the RAO, but he was not in his office. I was told that he was in my squadron.

When I went down to the squadron, he and the officer commanding were in a meeting. I spoke to the second in charge, instead. The first thing he said to me was, "This thing that you're doing, going round the regiment telling everyone that you are ill, it won't work. It is best if you just stop it, and just get on with your work."

"But, sir, I am ill. I am not pretending." By this time, I didn't have the fight in me anymore, so I asked him if I could return home for the day, which he granted, but he said I should go again to see the RAO, which I did.

It now seemed like I was going into a deeper hole; no one was listening to me, and I found myself getting even more ill. All sorts of thoughts and ideas were going through my mind, trying to put an end to what I was experiencing.

Before going home, I saw the RAO together with a sergeant, with whom, he told me, I would be working. The sergeant made it clear to me that I would start promptly at 8.00 am then go to lunch at 12.00 noon and leave at 5.00 pm starting the next day.

In my head, it was clear that the doctor hadn't said anything to them. It was obvious to me that they had concluded that I had been pretending to be ill, and made no attempt to support or listen to my cries for help in dealing with this depression.

I now felt a strong sense of shame and rejection. I called Michael to come and pick me up. I told myself that, one way or the other, there wasn't going to be a tomorrow over there, but I knew I wouldn't go AWOL, as they would have found me, and the situation would have been even worse for me.

When I arrived home, I thought that, since I wasn't being listened to by the doctor nor by the Det at work, it would be a good idea to speak to the commanding officer to get her to intervene for me. I reasoned that since she was a female like me, there was the likelihood that she would understand what I was going through. I was desperate for help.

Michael dialled the number. It rang several times but, as fate would have it, as soon as the adjutant answered it, and he and Michael had begun to talk, our phone went dead. He got a sergeant to order me to go back over to the camp to see him.

When I got there, I was put under so much pressure as he laid into me. "Do you know that the CO has a lot of things to do? What are you doing, getting your husband to call the CO? Do you want us to ban him from coming over here? He is already banned from the medical centre, and that will be bad for you, as he would have to drop you at the gate and you'd have to walk all the way down to the hangar to your squadron, and then walk back to the gate for him to pick you up again!"

Should I have asked Michael to call the CO? Perhaps that wasn't such a clever thing to do, but I was genuinely desperate. I was seeking to get someone with some clout to listen and understand what I had been going through. It wasn't that I wanted to go off work; I was terrified at the prospect of going back into that dark place of depression.

Michael continued to support me with care and sensitivity. When I arrived home, he took full control of the children, which allowed me to spend time by myself in bed without any disturbances.

This was my opportunity to take the steps to end all these problems I was causing them. While Michael and the children were in the living room, I was careful enough to leave the house in my nightie, robe and bed slippers. It was a few minutes after five in the afternoon in March.

I was heading to the woods near the disused Hullavington Airfield. A few metres away from my destination I saw my neighbour's mother, out walking with her friend. I was surprised to see anyone since it was such a cold evening.

"Necola! What are you doing out here, dressed like this? Where is Michael? Does he know that you are out here? Did you and Michael have a fuss?" she asked rapidly.

"No, not at all," I replied to her final question.

"Is it work again?" She was aware that my relationship with work had deteriorated since the accident.

Both women accompanied me back to the house. Michael said that he had just missed me, as he thought that I was still in bed, and was just about to call the police when I returned home.

For the first time, I saw that this whole episode was taking its toll on my husband. I felt like he thought he had failed to protect me.

I honestly could not believe what was happening to me. I had suffered from depression before, and had just been put back on medication by the psychiatrist, and still no one seemed to believe that my condition was genuine. I felt like it was Michael and me against this great Army, and they were using their position and authority to make my life a living hell. I had no one to talk to or to represent my interests. The doctors were just looking out for the interests of the regiment and, in so doing, had neglected their duty of care towards me.

Throughout the night, my mind kept running at an incredibly fast pace and I just couldn't shut it down. I replayed the events of the day repeatedly, which caused me to have a sunken feeling deep within. I remembered that Michael prayed for me, and tried to reassure me that things would be better, but at that moment in time, I just couldn't see any hope of things improving.

I couldn't sleep and neither could he. I had the impression that he was watching me closely to prevent me doing anything stupid. There was an incident, however, which prompted Michael to get in touch with the DCMH's out-of-hours service, who in turn contacted the Wiltshire out-of-hours service. They sent a doctor to our home to check on me.

Due to the state I was in, the doctor wrote a strongly worded letter to my GP, demanding that I be seen by the psychiatrist as soon as possible. When I arrived to see him, he immediately arranged for me to be admitted into hospital. I was sent to a hospital, which was located over one hundred and twenty miles from where I lived, all the way in Staffordshire.

I was devastated that my mental health had deteriorated to the point where I was being admitted to a mental hospital in Britain. This is exactly what I had wanted to avoid all along, but the people, who should have been caring for me, hadn't been listening to me.

I felt a deep sense of shame. I was also hurt and angry that I had been let down by an institution which prided itself on looking after its own. I had begged them to listen, but as far as I was concerned, no one cared about this Black private.

I also felt that I had let down my faith in Jesus Christ. I began to think that I was a weak Christian, as I had allowed these people to drive me to the point where I was in a mental institution.

It was difficult to consider myself a true Christian at this stage, and it was something that I grappled with for a considerable period of time. I was determined, though, that no matter what, I would never let go of my faith in Jesus Christ.

I told Michael that I didn't want the children to come and visit me in that hospital, as I didn't want them to see me looking so wild and vulnerable. He took them to see me on Mother's Day and until now that has been one of the worse days of my life. I often cringe when I remember the events of that day.

I had no visitors from the Army – neither from the Detachment nor the Welfare department – while I was in hospital. I only received one telephone call from that young doctor, after I had complained to the caseworker that no one from work had even called to find out how I was doing.

I spent six days in a mental hospital, which was one of the low points of my life. In my opinion, this could have been prevented if only I had been listened to and given the support I was crying out for. I got the impression, though, that I was being set up to be given an administrative discharge, on the grounds that I was unable to carry out my duties.

My care plan from the mental hospital specified that I should have follow-up care from the GP the following day. I must admit that I was intimidated by the way he had treated me, but I put on a brave face to go and see him, as he was the only doctor on duty. He knew that I had an appointment with him, but chose not to see me and only left a prescription and the sick note for me with the receptionist.

Since then, I always avoided seeing this doctor. I was careful to check with the receptionist in advance to prevent booking appointments when he was on duty.

A couple of weeks later, I felt as if the anti-depressants were not working, as I was still feeling unwell. I returned to the medical centre to explain to the GP how I was feeling. It was the regular doctor on duty, so I felt more comfortable in bringing this to her attention. To my surprise, though, she was a bit short-tempered and behaved very dismissively towards me. "It is not a happy pill, you know," she snapped. This caused me to feel dejected, abused and hurt. Putting things into perspective, I felt I was being persecuted for suffering from depression. It became all too clear to me that these people did not believe that I was genuinely ill.

Soon after this, my psychiatric care was taken out of the hands of the regiment at 9th Regiment RLC, and transferred to the DCMH at RAF Brize Norton, where I attended fortnightly counselling sessions, and received support from the doctors. Finally, I started to make small improvements, which would eventually enable me to return to work on a phased basis.

The irony was, however, that before my mental health had deteriorated to the point where I had to be admitted to a mental hospital, I had been asking for counselling sessions, but had been ignored by the doctors and by the Regiment.

Sadly, I now have to live with the stigma that I was admitted to a mental institution, but I will not allow this to dictate my life.

27

Despite the small improvements that I had been making since being treated by the team at the DCMH at RAF Brize Norton, it was still a difficult period for me. I was very fearful of going out in public. Simple things, such as hearing the phone or the doorbell ringing, would cause me to go into fits of anxiety. I was afraid to go shopping or even to take the children to school.

The psychiatric nurse at the DCMH was absolutely brilliant. She gave me sound instructions on how to rebuild my confidence, and how to block out the negative emotions that were causing me to react to people this way. One of the things she did was to ask what I enjoyed doing around the home. I told her that I loved to cook and to bake, especially making rock cakes with the children, as well as gardening. I can remember telling her that I had lost all interest in these activities, and had just been living from day to day.

She suggested, however, that I should try doing some gardening and that I would be amazed at how this would slowly help me to rebuild my self-esteem. I was reluctant to do this, as I was concerned about what the people at work would say if they saw me planting flowers, especially in the garden at the front of the house.

She was a feisty individual, however, and told me in no uncertain terms how to deal with them if I encountered any problems.

She became my great support and friend and, on one occasion, I remember jokingly telling her that she was my 'fix'. She was just a great person to be around. I was always excited to go to the sessions, because she didn't judge me, and I felt that she believed and understood exactly what I was going through.

While this was happening, I still found it difficult to connect with the Lord. Michael remained steadfast in prayer and worshipping God. He continued having devotions, even when I was not interested.

He consistently played gospel music around the house, and the children would be singing and dancing and playing drums. Michael often encouraged me to sing as he said that the singing would help me. I knew that everything he was saying was right but, at that time, I just could not do it. I knew, though, that I had a song in my heart at all times, but for some reason I just could not verbalise it.

Michael encouraged me to look after myself. He pointed out that if I started looking after myself and got better, then I would be able to care better for those who were dear to me, especially my children. He emphasised that he would continue to do the majority of the care of the children, which would allow me to get better gradually. The love and support that I received from my husband was phenomenal. I knew he was special, but it was when I was going through these challenging, personal difficulties, that he proved that he was indeed a gem. I often thanked his mother for her wonderful son. My childhood dream of marrying a good man was realised when I met and married Michael.

In fact, when I first saw this confident looking KC (Kingston College) boy looking at me on the old Jolly bus, plying the Kingston to Bull Bay route in Jamaica,

I hated him for even looking at me. "Oh no, not this one. You are just a user," I said angrily to myself. Oh how wrong I was; he has been a great tower of strength throughout our relationship and an absolute gentleman.

Initially, I felt confused that he was even interested in me, and when he got his first job at the bank I thought that was it now, I'd lost him to all those educated bank girls. When he started taking me to his work events, however, I felt more assured that he truly loved me. One day, before we got married, I visited him at work and he was called out of a meeting. Michael took me straight back to the meeting room, and introduced me to everyone as his fiancée. All his friends at the bank became my friends as well.

I am not sure if it was the depression or the anti-depressants – or a combination of the two – but all I knew was that I had no interest in sexual activity with my husband, but he was extremely patient with me. Sometimes for months we would not have any form of sexual contact, so when I got pregnant again – oh yes, again! – it was a surprise to both of us.

I felt frightened about what the people at work were going to say. I felt ashamed that I was pregnant again, especially while still on sick leave, and was terrified to go and see the doctor regarding this surprising news.

I was taking contraceptives yet I still got pregnant. I was later told by the doctor that the anti-depressants had probably nullified the effects of the contraceptive pills, thus resulting in this pregnancy, which was confirmed by the doctor at the medical centre on the camp.

One morning, when I was about ten weeks pregnant, I noticed that I was bleeding quite a lot. I became upset at the prospect of losing my child. Due to the excessive bleeding I was experiencing, I was referred to the Early Pregnancy Unit at the Royal United Hospital in Bath, and I went early the next morning. We decided that if we lost the child, it was God's will, however devastating this would have been. As the radiographer placed the probe on my abdomen, we held each other's hands and looked in hope at the monitor that we would see the little heartbeat. Yes! There it was; the baby was still in place despite the bleeding. I was overjoyed. "Thank You, Jesus," I muttered loudly, relieved that there were still signs of life.

We now had to start to make plans to receive another little member into our family.

This pregnancy was also a challenge; once again, I encountered the usual difficulties I had had during previous pregnancies. The pre-eclampsia had returned, as well as the SPD and, once again, the baby was breached from about twenty-six weeks into the pregnancy. I thought I managed much better on this occasion, though. Many people were surprised that I had a second breached pregnancy. We decided that we would call her Moriah, from the passage in Genesis 22.

The caesarean section was arranged for early June. I thought the Obstetrics team was brilliant, and their care and attention to detail were outstanding. Moriah was born ten minutes past four in the afternoon. She was beautiful and healthy and, for that, Michael and I were thankful to God for blessing us with our daughter.

To this day, I still have not had surgery to remove the fibroid, after three successful pregnancies. I still feel pain from it at times, but I have certainly not made it bigger than my God.

Just prior to going on maternity leave, I was posted to the Personnel Recovery Unit (PRU) in Tidworth to assist in my rehabilitation to return to work, or to be medically discharged from the Army.

I remember in December 2011, we had a visit to my home from the commanding officer from the PRU, accompanied by the personnel recovery officer. Michael and I had a frank and open discussion with them about how I had been treated by 9th Regiment RLC. Before they left, the CO commented that we had been harshly treated by the regiment.

In order to somehow make up for what we had endured, he suggested that we go on holiday to anywhere we wanted – at their expense. Michael and I looked at each other in utter disbelief. He suggested that we take a trip to see our families in Jamaica. We were both lost for words, but were encouraged by the CO to get the quotes for flights and a hire car, and to get back to them as swiftly as possible.

This was early December, and we agreed that it would have been great to go to Jamaica over the Christmas holidays. It was a frantic time organising everything, but we arrived in Jamaica via Miami and Montego Bay on December 9, and spent five weeks in the sun.

It was great to receive support from our respective families while in Jamaica. We had the rare chance to leave the children with them, so we could have some time alone for a break with each other at a hotel. This was what had been missing back in England, as it was just Michael and me with the children. Going through the challenges at work had made it very difficult for us to cope under the severe pressure we were put under.

I thought long and hard about my future, and the prospect that I might have to leave the Army. I was determined nonetheless to stay in the Army to prove to my detractors that I was competent in carrying out my duties as a military clerk if given the chance. I made up my mind that I would never quit.

Similarly, I was confident that I would soon be able to perform even if I had to return to work on a graduated basis.

The holiday to Jamaica came at a very good time for us. It was absolutely brilliant being there with the children over the Christmas season. This brought back a lot of memories when I was a child, and even the times spent with Michael in the early years of our relationship over Christmas. For me, there was no better placc to be during the Christmas holidays than Jamaica, especially now that I could leave the children with their grandmothers.

My reality was, however, that I now lived and worked in the UK, and I had better snap out of the holiday mood and prepare to go back to the job.

I returned to the UK in mid-January 2012. I was apprehensive, as I knew what lay ahead in terms of getting myself ready again to go back into the workplace. I had been on sick leave followed by maternity leave, which meant that I had been away from work for a considerable length of time. This was a daunting prospect, but somehow I believed I was up for the challenge.

I knew that I would be required to attend a medical board but, while I waited for the date for the board to be confirmed (and for its decision whether I was medically fit), there were a number of courses that I needed to complete before I would be deemed ready to return to work.

One such course was a residential course. I therefore had to leave the children with Michael to look after. I knew it would be a struggle for him to cope on his own, with a seven-month-old baby and two toddlers. Prior to going to Jamaica, Michael had

had to resign from his job to ensure that he was around to support me and the children. He did brilliantly well, looking after the children while I was away.

Nonetheless, I was extremely emotional while I was on the course. The other participants were soldiers, who had suffered serious physical injuries while on tour in Afghanistan, as well as soldiers who, like me, didn't present the physical wounds, but were mentally ill.

I felt angry at times, as care and attention were predominantly given to those with the physical wounds. At times, I felt sorry for them, even though they didn't want anyone's pity. On occasions, I felt that it would have been better to have been physically injured, as at least people would see and know that you were suffering. Later in the course, I realised that all the other personnel suffering with mental health issues shared a similar view to mine.

One of the modules that I had to do was the dyslexia screening. This was really nerve-racking for me; my main concern was what would this say about me?

I did the screening and realised that I was struggling to complete the questions and tasks in a timely manner. At the time, I didn't know if this was as a result of my mental state or something else. I felt that I was falling behind the required standard, and knew before I was even finished that the outcome would be dire. I felt mentally drained and physically exhausted.

Later in the afternoon, the facilitator called me in to advise me of the result of the dyslexia screening. Some people had said that they were given good results, so I was hoping for the same.

The facilitator informed me that, based on my results, I was showing traits of dyslexia. I had a sunken feeling in my stomach; I felt literally sick, and started to sob uncontrollably at receiving this information. Many things started playing over in my mind. I started to say that this was the reason why my colleagues were always saying that I was slow and lazy, and that I was 'crap' at my job. This confirmed that the problem was that I had been suffering from dyslexia, and needed more time to complete tasks. I was not lazy after all; in fact, I was a very hardworking individual who had been stereotyped and marginalised by incompetent managers, who had been quick to jump to conclusions about my abilities, without giving me the suitable level of support and opportunities for over nine years.

In my opinion, I had been singled out, humiliated and abused, while all this time if I had been assessed for dyslexia before, then more than likely my Army career would not have been on the verge of coming to an end. This career had been important to me on many levels. For me, this was what I had always wanted to do, and I had worked incredibly hard to have been accepted in the first place. Additionally, my career gave me the opportunity to be able to provide a decent standard of living for my children. It also provided the platform that would enable Michael and me to ensure that our children got the chance to receive quality education.

The assessor went on to ask questions about my childhood and educational background. This was too much for me to deal with at this time. She went on to ask if the words moved on the paper when I read. "Yes," I answered in astonishment. She then did a further assessment to see whether I had photoscopic sensitivity relating to reading. This test also found that I was positive, which indicated that I would benefit if I read written words with blue overlays. I was referred to an optician, who immediately prescribed a reading lens as well as a coloured lens. Before this, I had never worn glasses. I was totally and utterly surprised how different words and objects looked through the lens; it was like a brand new world had been opened to me.

Being given all this information about the dyslexia caused me to look back over my life and the challenges I had experienced, even to the point where I hadn't even sat the common entrance examination in Jamaica. This was an examination wherein children aged ten to twelve were tested before they were placed in high (secondary) school. I remember wanting so much to go the Wolmer's Girls School, as I normally drove past that school on the bus, on my way to my dad's workplace in New Kingston. I admired seeing the girls in their sky blue tunics with white blouses.

I began to question now if this was the reason, as far back as then, why I hadn't been put forward for this exam. I can also remember struggling when I did evening classes in Jamaica, in an effort to get some CXC passes that would have enabled me to get ahead. I had tremendous difficulties with many of the subject areas and even with taking dictation. I was often embarrassed that I was not able to keep up with the taking of notes, and was shunned by friends when I borrowed theirs.

Since being in the Army, I can remember that on one occasion the welfare officer at the last regiment had asked if I was dyslexic as a reason why I was unable to complete the jobs that I had been given to do. I was mortified at this question, and was robust in my rebuttal of him even asking. "No, sir" I replied emphatically, "I can do my job."

To a large extent, the result from this dyslexia screening had opened a floodgate of emotions for me. All along I had thought that I was slow due to the lack of attendance to school, but it further explained that, in addition, there was something else at play, which had contributed significantly to my lack of progress.

This begged the question, was I in denial? I genuinely didn't think I was. I had no idea that I suffered from this condition, and even now had started to wonder if there was a relationship between the dyslexia and my mental illness. I have no scientific evidence to support this, but I believe it was a factor.

I thank God for His hand on my life amidst the many difficulties, and for somehow holding me through those dark times when I didn't felt like I could live to face another day. In addition, He has been directing me, even to the point that I became a clerk in the Army, instead of a chef or supply specialist. It is likely that these roles would not have revealed these deficiencies, as I believe my mental abilities would not have been challenged in the same way. (No offense or disrespect intended.) I strongly believe the Scriptures that say, "And we know that all things work together for good to them that love God, to them who are called according to His purpose" (Romans 8:28 KJV).

I thank the British Army for giving somebody like me an opportunity to serve and to have a feeling of self-worth and personal achievement. I will always cherish the experiences – good and bad – and I hold no grudge or bitterness towards the people who mistreated me. On the whole, they have all contributed to me getting to this point in my life, where I am a stronger, confident and more resilient individual.

28

The journey of my own life often causes me to think about children who are suffering the same way I did some thirty years ago. There are children today in communities similar to the one that I grew up in Jamaica, whose parents have a totally twisted and irresponsible attitude towards the role that education should play in the lives of their children.

I am angry about this, as I am an example of how the lack of a fundamental level of education can cause limitation to one's ability to progress and compete for opportunities in the wider world.

There are still too many parents having children whom they cannot afford to send to school regularly, due to poverty. This is devastating for the children, and will result in the cycle of poverty repeating itself over and over again. I feel for the children who, like me, deserve a better opportunity in getting an education. It should not be left to chance whether a child advances in their education or not, without the specific nurturing and support of their parents.

I was determined to break that cycle, and was driven by ambition. Although I didn't receive the educational foundation I would have liked, I was driven to the point that I came to the United Kingdom in search of a better life, firstly for me and, most importantly, for the children that Michael and I would have in the future. I therefore seized the opportunity to join the Army when it came along. I have a passion to be successful, despite my apparent limitations.

I do believe that the circumstances of my childhood had a significant bearing on my adult life. I look back to the years when I didn't attend school for weeks, and how I felt when I returned: lost and totally out of place, and wanting to go back home to my mother to be comforted by her.

If I could go back thirty years or so, and see 'little me', I would just embrace her and tell her that everything was going to be fine. Despite the many challenges ahead, Jesus Christ is in control of her life, and He will protect, lead and comfort her, and she doesn't have to be fearful about the future.

I give God all the glory.